HAUNTED
TAMPA

13 Haunted Locations in Tampa Bay

Gare Allen

100% of the net proceeds of the sale of this book will be donated to the HCSO Deputy Dogs, The Hillsborough County Sheriff's Office K-9 Unit, in support of local law enforcement and their canine partners.

Thank you for all that you do.

Other books by Gare Allen:

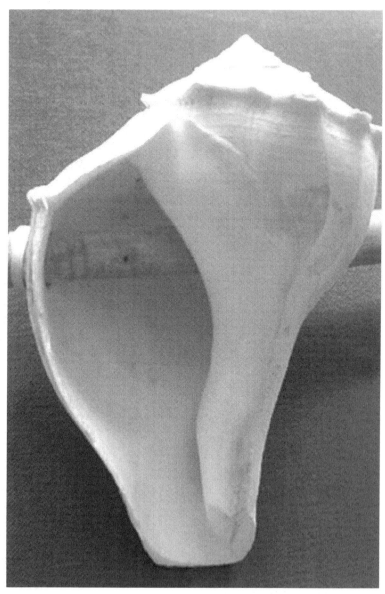

A Calusa hammer fashioned with a shell

Chapter One
The Shell People

Inside one of Tampa's finest neighborhoods resides a couple with a story that has ties to Tampa's early beginnings. In the interest of privacy, we will refer to them only as Sandra and David.

The couple married in the spring of 1981 and then purchased their first home together the following year. Both intent on living near the water, the historic neighborhood of Beach Park promised to be a perfect find. Built to attract a certain class of people, eighty of the stunning original homes still remain. David described their first visit to the house.

"We pulled up to the house and were immediately taken in by the strong Mediterranean influence of the architecture. The terra cotta roof, stucco exterior and large windows immediately catapulted us to Spain. The palm trees, large Oak trees and azaleas provided a lush background to a stunning structure. A hint of salt air from Tampa Bay wafted through the air. In all honesty, we were sold on it before we ever saw the inside of the home."

Sandra described their initial time inside the house. "The air conditioner wasn't on, so entering the home was like walking into a wall of heat. However, the uncomfortable climate quickly lost our attention as we walked through the interior archways that connected the rooms. Beneath us was an endless path of colorful, patterned tiles. They boasted so many colors and designs that I almost got dizzy staring at their beauty. Halfway through the tour David caught my eye and we exchanged a glance. Without words, we told one another that we were home."

After living just one week in their Beach Park home, Sandra's sister, Sarah, took full advantage of the opportunity to visit Florida. Leaving behind the cold air of Chicago, Sarah and her ten-year-old daughter Angela flew down to spend a few days in The Sunshine State.

"I had taken some time off from work to get the house settled while David was out of town for his work. I was a little nervous about being in a new home all alone so my sister's visit was more than welcomed. Angela and Sarah arrived around noon on a Tuesday." Sandra laughed as she recalled her niece's first words upon entering her house. "Angela gave me a big hug and then immediately asked, 'When are we going swimming?' I showed them to the guest room and they put their suitcases on the bed with the intention of unpacking later on in the day. I had already made sandwiches for lunch but Sarah was so anxious to see the water that I packed them and a few towels into a bag and we all headed for Tampa Bay."

The sisters spent the day sitting along the shoreline, talking and catching up with each other's lives. Sarah kept one motherly eye on Angela as she split her time between playing in the shallow edges of the water and endlessly searching for seashells.

"Look at this one, Mommy!" For hours Sarah smiled and nodded in approval at Angela's latest treasure find.

When the bright Florida sun began to set beneath the watery horizon, they headed back to Sandra's house for dinner.

"My sister and niece were exhausted from their travel and time in the sun. After dinner we all got cleaned up and called it an early night. Sarah and Angela retired to the guest room and unpacked. A little later I visited them to make sure they had everything they needed for the night. Sarah was already half asleep in the bed while Angela was meticulously placing her prized seashells on top of the dresser. She had chosen a half dozen or so that she thought were just perfect enough to make her friends back home so very jealous of her vacation to Florida. Finally, she climbed into bed with her mother. I made a point to close the curtains so that the morning sun didn't wake them up too early in case they wanted to sleep in. Then, I told them goodnight and turned out the light. A few minutes later I was fast asleep in my own bedroom and the night passed without incident."

Sandra woke up early the next morning to the sound of her sister and niece having a loud verbal exchange. As she made her way toward their room she could just make out their words.

"Where did they go?"

"Angela, are you sure you put them on the dresser?"

"Yes! They were all right here!" Angela placed her hand on the top of the empty dresser. She then scoured the floor, convinced that her missing shells must have surely fallen during the night.

"Look in your bag, maybe you put them in there."

"Mom, I know *for a fact* that I put them on top of the dresser!"

Sandra walked into the guest room and began looking for her niece's shells. "I saw you put them on top of the dresser last night. Did you go back and move them?"

Angela was becoming upset. "No! I went to sleep and now they're gone!"

Sandra placed her hand on Angela's head and smiled. "It's alright. We'll go back today and get some more." She turned to her sister. "Right?"

Sarah smiled. "Of course." She turned her head away from the bright sunlight coming through the window. "I have to remember to close the curtains tonight."

Sandra thought to herself, I thought I had closed them?

The girls ate breakfast and then repeated the previous day's events. They packed a lunch and spent the entire day along the water. Angela scrutinized every shell she came across and played along the edge of the water until sunset.

Later at the house they ate dinner and played card games. When it was time for bed, Angela placed her shells along the top of the dresser in a perfect line.

"I found ten today!"

Her mom smiled and closed the curtains over the window. Soon they both were fast asleep.

The next morning, Sandra awoke to the same voices having the same conversation. She hurried to the guest room to find her niece in tears.

"Someone took my shells again!"

Sandra looked at her sister in confusion. "Where did they go?"

Sarah threw her hands up in frustration. "I don't know. They were on the dresser when we went to bed, I saw them! And, now they're gone...again!"

They looked behind the dresser, under the bed and inside the drawers but there was no sign of the shells. Angela began crying and hugged her mother.

Sarah stroked her daughter's hair in comfort and arched an eyebrow at Sandra. "I guess it's another day on the water." She squinted at the sunlight streaming through the window, released by the open curtains. "Angela, did you open the curtains?"

"No. They were open when I woke up."

Sarah looked at her sister in confusion but neither spoke.

"The third day was like déjà vu." Sandra explained. "We had breakfast, packed a lunch and spent the remainder of the day's light along the water. This time, Angela collected over twenty shells. She said she was trying to make up for the ones that vanished. So, fast forward to later that night. Just like the previous nights, she arranged her shells neatly on top of the dresser and went to bed. In fact, we all went to bed a little earlier that night because my sister and niece were flying back to Chicago and had to be to the airport quite early." Sandra's eyes widened and she shook her head. "But, no one got any rest that night. Especially Angela."

Around two o'clock in the morning, Sandra was startled out of her slumber by the terrifying scream of her niece. She ran to the guest room where her hand scanned the inside wall for the light switch. When the light filled the room she saw her niece crying and in her mother's protective embrace. After a few minutes, Angela calmed down to the point where she could explain what had upset her.

Sandra sat down on the edge of the bed. "Tell me what happened, Angela."

"I saw a man!"

Sandra sprang up off of the bed. "Where?"

"He was standing where you are right now!"

"Where did he go?"

She pointed toward the dresser. "He walked through that wall."

Sandra relaxed a bit as her mind determined her fears to be the result of a bad nightmare.

"What did he look like?"

"He was tall with really long hair."

Angela's mom spoke softly. "I think you had a nightmare, Sweetie."

"No, he was real. He's the one who took my shells." She pointed again toward the dresser. "See, they're gone."

The sisters looked in unison at the top of the dresser to confirm Angela's statement. The shells were once again missing.

Sandra noticed the open curtains of the bedroom window. Her sister followed her line of sight and anticipated her query. "Yes, I closed those when we went to bed."

Sandra ran her finger across the lock, confirming it was secure. She ran room to room and checked all of the doors and windows in her house. There was no sign of a break-in, no unlocked entryways and nothing had been disturbed. Except, of course, the mystery of the missing shells and the open curtains. Soon, Angela calmed down and they managed some broken sleep off and on for a few more hours until it was time leave for the airport.

Sarah and Angela left for the airport leaving Sandra alone in her home. David was scheduled to fly back later that same day but she still felt uneasy about being home by herself. To keep her thoughts off of being alone and enjoy the beautiful day that Tampa had gifted her, she decided to work in her backyard. First, she weeded a small flower garden that boasted various vibrant perennials.

Next, she raked the dried leaves that rested beneath a stunning old Oak tree. As she raked the leaves into small piles she heard the sound of metal scraping against a hard surface. She raked a few more leaves to uncover the source of the sound. Her jaw dropped. Sandra described what she found.

"Beneath the leaves were dozens of shells. Angela's shells! I couldn't believe what I was seeing. They weren't thrown on the ground, they had to have been put there, underneath all those leaves. How that happened I have no idea!"

Sandra collected the shells and boxed them. A few days later she sent them to her niece in Chicago. About a week after that, she received a call from Sarah.

"Hi, Sandra. Thank you for sending the shells to Angela. She was so happy to get them. At first, anyway."

Sandra was confused. "What do you mean, *at first*?"

"This is going to sound crazy but she put the shells on her dresser, just like she did when we stayed with you." She paused.

"And?"

"Well, she had the same nightmare about the tall man with the long hair. She saw him in her bedroom and it terrified her."

"What has that got to do with the shells?"

"She's convinced the man in her nightmare wanted her shells. It scared her so much that she said she was going to throw them away."

"Sarah, I'm so sorry. If I knew sending them would upset her, I wouldn't have sent them."

"Oh, it's not your fault. And, she didn't really throw them away."

"What do you mean?"

"I found them under a tree in the backyard. I guess she changed her mind or something."

Sandra gasped and made an excuse to quickly end the call. She sat down on her sofa to contemplate how her sister's words made the hairs on her arms stand up although at the time she wasn't sure why.

Eventually she put the whole experience out of her mind. Years passed and Sandra and David enjoyed their amazing home together, as well as the year-round outdoor living that Florida offers. Sandra had all but forgotten about the shells until one day when she attended a local community event. The guest speaker was an expert on local Native American history. She found the subject matter interesting and decided to attend the event.

The orator spoke of several Native American tribes that once flourished in Florida including the Choctaw, Timucua and Miccosukee. Sandra listened as he talked about their way of life and how they flourished and expanded across the lush state of Florida. But when he began to describe the Calusa people, Sandra found herself frozen in her chair. Sandra recalls the speaker's words.

"First he told us about the geographic location of the Calusa."

The Calusa inhabited the southwest coast from Tampa Bay to Cape Sable. With approximately fifty villages, they numbered over three-thousand in the mid 1600's. One of those villages was called Tanpa, meaning Stick of Fire, most likely referring to the vast amount of lightning that still fills the Tampa sky. Later, perhaps through poor cartography or illegible writing, the spelling was changed to Tampa.

"While that part was interesting, the next bit of information was jarring."

The Calusa men were tall, fierce warriors with long hair.

"I immediately recalled Angela's description of the man she claimed she saw in my guest room. Given Beach Park's proximity to the coastline where they once hunted for food, could she have seen the ghost of a Calusa man?"

The Calusa men and boys would hunt for fish while the woman and girls searched for shellfish like conch and oysters. Once eaten, they used the shells for tools like saws and fishing net weights.

"My mind continued to weave a pattern to the events in my home. Did a spirit of a Calusa man visit us? Was he attracted to the shells that he once used for tools and weapons?"

A typical Calusa home was built on stilts with palmetto branch roofs but they did not construct walls leaving an open viewpoint of the village.

"Despite our intentional closing of the curtains in the guest room, they were opened each night as we slept. Was the spirit creating an open viewpoint?" Sandra paused. "But, why would he put the shells under a tree?"

In 2017 Hurricane Irma severely damaged parts of the southwest coastline of Florida. Along its path, the storm unearthed multiple Royal Poinciana and Gumbo Limbo trees, pulling their roots and surrounding dirt out of the ground. The strong winds had unearthed artifacts of the Calusa people, including pottery, glass, tools and shells.

Sandra says that while she can never be sure, she believes her niece was visited by the spirit of a Calusa Native American. After learning about the Calusa's rich history in Tampa she often collects shells and places them under the large oak tree in her backyard in their honor.

A stunning nighttime shot of Tampa Theatre

Chapter Two
10,000 Stars

When Tampa Theatre opened in 1926, the cost to see a movie was only a quarter. While the price of admission has certainly changed, much of the landmark's history still lives on, some of it in haunting spirit.

Tampa Theatre's grand design was intended to attract massive amounts of moviegoers and provide a cinematic experience like none other at the time. Architect John Eberson achieved this endeavor with fifteen hundred seats, a balcony and by using an eclectic display of décor.

As you walk across the stunning terrazzo floor, you feel the cold glares of the theatre's stone, stoic gargoyles perched in protection of their home. The interior surrounds you with tapestries, paintings and dozens of mirrors. Looking up, a blue sky stretches across the ceiling. Its beauty only magnifies when hundreds of single bulbs display themselves as twinkling stars. Originally, there were ten thousand bulbs burning above visitor's heads.

For decades, Tampa Theatre was wildly popular and became an adored landmark, but increased costs and the widespread acquisition of home televisions drastically reduced the movie theatre audience. The once thriving theatre was in danger of being closed down. However, in 1973, the community of Tampa and its officials came together to save their beloved theatre.

Over the years the venue has had many employees and volunteers. It's reported that some of them have stuck around even after their employment and life had ended.

In 1930, Foster "Fink" Finley manned the projector at Tampa Theatre. Like one of the hanging tapestries, he was a fixture in the venue. For thirty-five years he fed film into the machine, kept the lens clean and projected a beam of comedy, drama and action movies and supplying hours of entertainment for his community. Sadly, in 1965, while a movie played out on the massive screen,

Fink suffered a heart attack in the projection booth and passed away.

Since his passing, workers have reported strange and unexplainable events including personal items being moved from one place to another.

Fink's successor told the story of feeling pushback on the other side of the door leading into the projector booth. Assuming someone was wanting entry, he pulled the door open to reveal that no one was there.

A long term employee also had an experience that left him jarred. While working alone in one part of the theatre, he found that his personal belongings had gone missing. Unable to find them, he considered the theatre's reputation for being haunted and asked, out loud, for his items to be returned. He turned his head and his belongings had appeared behind him. He gasped and stared in amazement while his mind struggled to reconcile what had happened.

Another employee claims to have been tapped on his shoulder by an unseen finger, several times over the course of thirty minutes. Each time he felt a tap he turned around to find no one behind him. For days, he kept one eye over his shoulder expecting it to happen again.

Frequently, instances of walking through freezing cold spots and feeling the presence of someone are reported. Francis, a young female visiting the theatre, reported that when she walked through a hallway she felt a rush of cold air against her face. At the same moment, she felt a strong hand caress her neck. She screamed and ran out of the theatre.

More than a few times, the sound of doors opening and closing on their own can be heard by employees working alone and with no explanation. On occasion, cigarette smoke can be seen coming out of the projection booth window. Fink was well known to be a smoker.

Currently, Tampa Theatre is being managed by the not-for-profit Tampa Theatre Foundation. The historic venue boasts over six-hundred events a year including concerts, special events, corporate events, classic and first-run movies and educational programs. Despite their success, forty percent of their income to remain affordable and accessible to everyone is made through contributions to the Tampa Theatre Foundation. But make no mistake, Tampa Theatre is rich in history, rich in elegance and definitely rich in spirit.

Ballast Point

Chapter Three
Boats on the Bay

Before the mansions and elegant homes in the neighborhood of Ballast Point sprouted up along the Bay waters of Tampa, the area was home to an American Civil War skirmish. As a result the event has sparked paranormal activity.

Paranormal author Sam Baltrusis explains: "Based on my experience as a paranormal researcher and author of eight historical-based ghost books, a battle like the skirmish in Tampa can create what experts call an 'aura of disaster,' or an environment that triggers ghostly happenings. I see it all the time in New England, specifically in areas that had a past-life as a battlefield. The event leaves a psychic imprint on the location and sensitives like myself can pick up on the lingering energy. *The Stone Tape Theory usually applies to battlefields as well and I've experienced first-hand residual energy replaying itself like a video-taped recording."

*The Stone Tape theory is the speculation
that ghosts and hauntings are analogous to tape recordings, and
that mental impressions during emotional or traumatic events
can be projected in form of energy, "recorded" onto rocks and
other items and "replayed" under certain conditions.

The Battle of Ballast Point took place on October 18, 1863. A Union raiding party led by Acting Master T. R. Harris disembarked at Ballast Point, landing at the current intersection of what is now Gandy Boulevard and Bayshore Boulevard. Under the protracted diversionary bombardment of the city of Tampa and Fort Brooke by two ships, the *USS Tahoma* and the *USS Adela*, the Union divisions marched fourteen miles to the Hillsborough River near the site of today's Lowry Park Zoo. They attacked and burned two ships, the *Scottish Chief* and the *Kate Dale*. Barely escaping, James McKay and members of his crew fled to warn the landing party.

After the ships burned, the Confederate forces found the raiding party's location. Harris's Union forces were surprised by a detachment of the garrison, the 2nd Florida Infantry Battalion. A brief exchange ensued before the Union troops returned to sea.

In the end, three Union and twelve Confederate soldiers lost their lives.

Today, thousands of people comprise the neighborhood of Ballast Point, including Janice and Rick. Married for just over twenty eight years, they bought their Ballast Point home in 1996. Built in 1956, the dwelling was admittedly small compared to the more modern homes they passed as they drove down their street. To Janice and Rick, it was just perfect. Inside their small, eighteen-hundred square-foot single-story home, they raised their two beautiful children. After years of birthday parties, soccer games and dances, their parenting efforts finally resulted in two honor students moving out and going off to college. With their space, and more importantly, their time to themselves, they immediately purchased a boat.

Their twenty-eight foot Boston Whaler had more than enough room for their friends as they spent almost every weekend on the water.

Janice recalls her children's reaction. "NOW you get a boat?"

Rick laughed and added, "The boat was a gift to ourselves. We didn't want to spend the money until we knew that the kids were set up for an education. Once that happened, we pulled the trigger."

While the couple had always gotten along well with their neighbors, there were some who disapproved of their boat being stored along the side of their home.

"I understand that having a boat visible from the street can reduce curb appeal and even go against community guidelines but the cost of storing a boat is significant." Rick explained. "About a year ago our neighbors approached us about storing the boat and I tried to explain that we really couldn't afford it at the time. But, they were adamant that we remove it from our property."

Janice added, "They would give us dirty looks and point at us and the boat while throwing their arms into the air in frustration."

"One Friday night in October, we had a pretty big scare." Rick clenched his teeth in anger while recalling the event. "It was late at night, a little after midnight I think and we were reading and about to go to bed. Suddenly, we heard three loud bangs on the front door. We both jumped up off the couch. My heart was pounding.

I told Janice to stay where she was and I went to the front door. Just before I opened it, there were three more loud bangs on the door.

They weren't knocks with a fist, it was like someone was hitting the door with a giant rock. And, as it happened the door almost came off of its hinges. My fear melted away to anger and I swung the door open."

Mike paused and shrugged his shoulders. "There was no one there. I ran outside and looked everywhere but there was no sign of anyone having been there. The cars weren't disturbed and the boat was fine. The motion sensor security lights didn't even come on until I walked outside and triggered them. It's crazy because I opened the door right after they banged on it the second time. There's no way anyone could have moved that fast."

The same thing happened the next night.

"Again, it was late and we were reading on the couch in the living room. It was around midnight and we heard three loud bangs on the front door. I ran to the door and waited. As soon as I heard another bang I opened the door." Rick shook his head. "Again, there was no one was there. No sign of anyone in the yard, the security lights hadn't been tripped, just nothing."

The next day Rick and Janice went out on the boat.

"It was a beautiful day and must have been out there for six or seven hours. We fished, chatted with our friends and even ate lunch on the water. Later that night after we had gotten cleaned up and had dinner, we fell asleep on the couch. And then, the banging was back. But this time it was ten times louder.

I was in a deep sleep so I was groggy when I made my way to the door. I happened to glance at the clock in the kitchen and it was just after midnight. The banging was so loud that I thought for sure the front door was going to come off its hinges. It was so loud that it was hurting my ears. The pounding was like a bomb going off over and over. It was deafening and sounded angry or something. I had one hand over my left ear when I got to the door. I turned for a second and saw Janice was behind me. I swung the door open and we both just stood there. I couldn't move. I don't know if I was frozen in fear or actually paralyzed but I couldn't move my legs, arms, nothing!"

"It was the same for me." Janice interjected. "I was looking over Rick's shoulder but I couldn't move any part of my body. And it was cold. Like, freezing cold. Which made no sense because we had just enjoyed an eighty degree day on the water."

Rick continued. "I'm looking out into the darkness and my eyes are adjusting. Slowly, three figures start to form in the darkness next to our boat. It seemed like minutes but it was only seconds that I saw them but I swear they were wearing Civil War soldier clothing. They had dark coats with light colored pants and these old looking rifles. Mike paused while recalling the terrifying incident. "They just stood there, staring at me. And then, they vanished. The cold air changed to warm, Florida humidity and I could move again."

Janice was nodding her head in agreement. "I saw the same thing. Three soldiers just standing there, next to our boat. Suddenly, they disappeared. As soon as I could move again, I screamed. We called the police but there was no sign of anyone having been in our yard."

Rick concluded the story. "It wasn't until we did some research on the Civil War and specifically the Battle of Ballast Point that it made sense. I believe the spirits of those Union soldiers came to us because of our boat. The night we saw them it was October 18, the anniversary of the battle."

Rick and Janice took another look at their budget and found an affordable boat storage unit within the week.

Tampa Airport Post Office

Chapter Four

Heavenly Help

According to paranormal investigator and author Joni Mayhan, ghosts often haunt places where they frequented while they were alive. In fact, personal items that held great value to the living can develop attachments after the person has died.

"If someone sent a letter to a loved one that was never received, I can easily see the spirit of that person hanging around the post office to look for it," said Mayhan.

Mayhan had personal experiences with a post office she worked at in Massachusetts. While working there, she worked under a long term postmaster. The woman always closed the post office for two hours during the lunch hour. After consuming a quick lunch, she would spend the remainder of the break napping on a cot in the back of the small town post office. Workers coming in during that period always knew to listen for the sounds of her snores. If they heard them, they were extra quiet. After the postmaster passed away, several postal workers were surprised that when they came in on their lunch break, they often heard the unmistakable sound of the former postmaster snoring. As soon as they moved towards the room where the cot once stood, the sounds instantly stopped. It was apparent the postmaster was still on duty. Death apparently didn't change a thing.On January 26th, 1775, Congress established the United States Post Office and named Benjamin Franklin as the first Postmaster General. While certainly another blatant act of the colony's growing independence, the decision was initially fueled by The Royal Postal Service's inability to reliably deliver William Goddard's *Pennsylvania Chronicle* to its readers. Goddard laid out a plan for a Constitutional Post to Congress citing the necessity of a punctual delivery of critical and time-sensitive news.

As Postmaster General, Franklin formed much of the structure for the mailing system including routes and standardized rates, accounting for weight, size and distance. At the time this book is being written, we are able to send a birthday card to anywhere in the United States for only forty-nine cents. While that may sounds inexpensive, keep in mind that in 2017, the United States Post Office delivered just under one-hundred and fifty billion pieces of mail.

Tampa's USPS mail and distribution facility at the Tampa International Airport was constructed in the early 1970's. Each day the mail arrives, the mail is sorted and the mail is sent out for delivery. Like other postal plants, it's a three-hundred and sixty-five days a year operation. The facility employs hundreds of workers of whom several have witnessed a paranormal experience while at work. Some of them shared their stories with me.

In the early 1980's, a longtime worker named Richard suddenly passed away in his sleep. His co-workers remarked of his friendly demeanor and generous smile. Working the early morning shift starting at five o'clock, Richard was known for his unwavering punctuality. Without fail, he would arrive every morning at four-thirty. A few days after his passing, a few of the workers who worked with Richard were still mourning the loss of their co-worker and friend. One morning a supervisor called them into a room to verbally counsel them regarding punching in before their scheduled shift began. Confused, one of the workers replied, "What are you talking about? I punch in at five o'clock every morning I work." One by one, the other workers nodded and added, "Me, too."

The supervisor rolled his eyes and dropped their time cards on the desk in front of them. "Explain this, then."

As each worker reviewed their time card, they gasped at what they saw. The day that Richard has passed away, each of them had timestamps that punched them in at exactly four-thirty in the morning. They looked at one another and smiled.

"Well?" The impatient supervisor asked.

One worker's eyes misted as she looked at her supervisor and spoke. "Even on his last day, he was still here on time."

*****

Hammond, a former manager, shared a strange experience that both bewildered him and warmed his heart.

On a normal work day, Hammond was contacted by a distraught father with an unusual request. He explained that his fourteen year-old son, Greg, had been sent to run two errands for his grandmother. Having just lost her husband, she now relied heavily on her grandson for assistance. Greg has always been close to his grandparents and truly enjoyed helping out his Grandma. She asked him to mail a letter and also purchase her a gallon of milk and a carton eggs. She supplied Greg with a five dollar bill for the groceries and a stamped envelope addressed to her sister that contained a letter thanking her for the flowers she had sent.

Greg happily made his way to the local store and stopped one block early to dispense the letter into the blue, corner mail collection box. The second it left his hand and fell into the box, he cringed, for the five dollar bill accompanied it. By design, human arms are unable to retrieve dispensed mail from the blue boxes but he desperately tried, nonetheless. Failing to reclaim the money, he recalled a conversation he had overheard about how tight money would be for his Grandma since the passing of her husband. Distraught and on the verge of tears, he ran home to enlist the help of his father.

Greg's father called Hammond and explained the situation. Hammond considered his steps and agreed to assist the father and son.

Hammond reviewed the day's route schedules and determined that the carrier collecting mail from the box in which Greg dropped the letter and money would be back to the plant around six o'clock in the evening. He asked them to come to that plant at that time.

Greg's father apologized repeatedly and thanked Hammond for his help.

Hammond dumped a large bag filled with hundreds of letters in front of them. "No problem. I can't let you touch the mail but I'll sort through it until I find the money."

For what seemed like an eternity, Greg and his father watched as Hammond picked through the letters in the massive pile of mail on the floor.

Finally, Hammond stood up and placed his hands on his hips. "Guys, I'm sorry but I don't see any five dollar bill."

Greg's father clenched his jaw and turned to his son. "Are you telling the truth? Did you really lose that money?"

Greg's eyes widened and the tone of his voice elevated. "Yes. I put it in the box with the letter."

His father narrowed his eyes. "If you're lying to me-"

"I'm not! I swear!" Greg interrupted as tears began to fall from his eyes.

Hammond offered another option to finding the money. "Well, let me get this mail into the letter sorting machine and we'll know for sure if it's in this pile."

Greg's father nodded in agreement and then looked down at his son. "Boy, you better be telling the truth."

Greg crossed his arms in a defiant pouting pose and mumbled, "Grandpa would believe me if he was still here."

With the assistance of the carrier, Hammond dumped the mail into the letter sorting machine's dispensary. One by one, the letters were individually sorted by mechanical finger and moved along the intricate conveyer system of the loud machinery.

They watched as the last of the letters were processed. The carrier lowered his head and looked sympathetically at Greg while Hammond turned to Greg's father. "I'm sorry, it doesn't appear that-"

"Grandpa!" Greg pointed and smiled through his tears. Following Greg's finger, his father and Hammond observed nothing in the nearby corner.

A loud rattling emanated from the letter sorting machine and the men turned their heads to witness the last thing they expected to see. Something shot high into the air and above the machine. They watched as a small green piece of paper slowly floated like a feather and landed at Greg's feet. Their mouths fell open as their eyes identified the paper as a five dollar bill.

Greg looked down, picked up the money and turned back to the empty corner. "Thanks, Grandpa."

El Círculo Cubano de Tampa

Chapter Five
Residual Replay

As paranormal researchers and investigators continue to gather evidence to help define the metaphysical aspects of ghosts, they have secured some strong evidence regarding spiritual activity. Residual hauntings are believed to be a replay of events that occurred when a ghost was in human form. An emotionally charged imprint is left behind and replayed in our world. They tend to play out like a television clip that's caught in a loop. For instance, if someone walked a specific path over and over again, it would be fairly normal to see them walking that same path. These residual hauntings seem to be especially frequent when the passing was sudden or traumatic. A building doesn't necessarily need to have decades of history to display residual hauntings, but they are often reported more frequently in structures with a long history. Incidentally, Tampa has several such places.

Renowned as one of the Travel Channel's Top Ten Most-Haunted Places in the United States is
El Circulo Cubano de Tampa which translates to *Circle of Cubans*. Locally it's known as Ybor City's Cuban Club. Additionally, it was declared haunted in a 2009 episode of *Ghost Hunters* by the show's paranormal investigators.

The original Cuban Club burned down in 1916 but a new, more elaborate, club emerged atop its embers a year later. Built in 1917 as a social gathering place for Cuban immigrants, this historic site just celebrated its centennial. In grand style, the building's decor boasts imported tile, stained glass and murals. The building once included a spa, ballroom, pharmacy, swimming pool, bowling alley and cantina.

During the 1960's, membership waned and the club declined in popularity and fortune. In 1992, the Cuban Club Foundation was created to save the building. It's now a nonprofit organization dedicated to preserving the beauty and history of the structure.

Ghost hunters, professional and amateur, volunteers and visitors seeking a scare have reported similar paranormal experiences that can be traced back to the club's history.

Reports of a little boy running and chasing a ball where the swimming pool used to be are a common occurrence. Investigators researched the history of the building and learned that a young boy named Jimmy accidentally drowned in the club's pool during its early history.

Alternatively, there were other deaths that have been categorized as quite intentional.

It's been reported that during the 1920's a struggling actor was performing on stage in the club's theatre and committed suicide before the entire audience. His spirit has been seen walking across the stage as well as in the bathroom. One woman reported that during a quick visit to the restroom to adjust her lipstick she found herself staring at the reflection of a man looming behind her. She screamed but when she turned around the man had vanished. A struggling actor desperate for an audience while alive now haunts the club, still vying for attention.

The Cuban Club also has an intriguing haunting that spills secrets from the past. Former club president El Fumador wasn't perceived to be an all-around good man. Known to be temperamental and abrasive his temper reached new heights when accused of skimming money by several board members. Their accusations fueled a conflict that escalated beyond words and El Fumador was killed. The murder was never brought to the courts and even El Fumador's final resting place is not documented. One person reporting the sighting of El Fumador also said they felt the sensation of someone's finger caressing their face. El Fumador was shot directly in the face. His antics only begin there. Reports of being pushed in the back and even slapped on the back of the head suggest El Fumador is just as cantankerous in death as he was in life.

Another ghost that is seen frequently is the apparition of a woman. Both guests and staff have been witness to this woman over the years. She is always seen wearing an elegant white dress with shiny red heels. While the specifics of her passing are uncertain, she walks the halls and glides up the staircase as she may have done repeatedly during her human lifetime.

Invisible fingers play the club's piano, sending mystical sounds throughout the club as a reminder that the living are not alone.

Due to the death surrounding the club, paranormal researchers have branded it with the nickname, Club Dead.

The energy in the club is heavy with residual hauntings of little Jimmy playing out his last day, the woman in the white dress continuously strutting her beauty up and down the stairs and a forgotten musician still playing songs from the past on the old piano.

Alternatively, intelligent hauntings accompany the paranormal activity as seen by the apparition of the suicidal actor. The bullying pushes and slaps of the murdered El Fumador remind all that visit that he still feels that he is in charge.

Old Florida Brewery Company

Chapter Six
The Elixir of Eternal Youth

In the sixteenth century, Spanish explorer Juan Ponce de Leon searched for the fabled fountain of youth. Native Americans in Florida spoke of such a magical water being located on the mythical land of Bimini. Presumed to be northwest toward the Bahamas, Juan set sail on his quest. Since Juan is not with us today, it's a safe assumption that fabled fountain was never found. At least by him.

Today, we may have something close to an elixir of eternal youth, at least in spirit. For many of us Floridians, nothing makes us feel ten years younger and ten feet taller than a locally brewed beer. Luckily, there are an ample amount of breweries, one even dates back to the late 1800's.

The Florida Brewing Company was founded in 1896 by Edward Manrara and Vicente Martinez Ybor. Ybor City is named for this legendary cigar industrialist who founded the city and was populated by thousands of immigrants from Italy, Spain and Cuba.

Born in Spain in 1819, Ybor immigrated to Cuba at the age of fourteen. Armed with an entrepreneur's heart, he became a cigar manufacturer in Cuba, Key West and eventually Tampa.

Built on the Government Spring, the area was rich in Native American legend. Many tribes including Florida's Paleo Native Americans believed the water in the spring to be sacred and possess healing properties. The belief was so widespread that the land surrounding the spring became a peace zone. Out of respect for the holiness of the water, the tribes would observe a peaceful interaction with each other.

Florida Brewing Company has the distinction of being the first brewery in the state of Florida. In 1897 it launched its La Tropical line and was once the leading exporter of beer to Cuba. At one time it produced eighty-thousand barrels of beer annually.

A celebration of the opening of the brewery provided of course, ample amounts of beer. It's told that a fight broke out between two drunk men shortly after the brewery first opened. One of the men was killed when he was struck in the head. Reports of voices are common throughout the building. One woman working late distinctly heard a man slurring his words in Spanish. Startled, she searched the building but found no one else.

The Florida Brewing Company successfully weathered both Prohibition and the Great Depression. However, the embargo on Cuba and the market muscle of Anheuser-Busch and Schlitz Brewing Company finally forced them to close down in 1961.

The building had a few more incarnations as storage for tobacco and later a bomb shelter during the Cold War. In 1999 it was converted and is currently a law firm and office space.

Despite the building's renovation, spirits still linger. Another worker reported that after returning to their desk, they would find all the paperwork had been scattered across their office floor. As they cleaned up the mess, deep snickering was heard from behind them. They turned but the sound stopped and there was no one there.

The William Bisbee aka The Jose Gaspar

Chapter Seven
A Pirate's Life

Tampa's identity most certainly contains nautical history from the over four-hundred square mile Tampa Bay. A large natural harbor that's connected to the Gulf of Mexico, its shallow depth measures an average of only twelve feet.

Extending along the coastlines of Hillsborough, Manatee and Pinellas counties, Tampa Bay boasts over two-hundred species of fish beneath its waves. In addition, countless playful dolphins and serene manatees are often a highlight of onlookers enjoying the bay's aquatic life. Above Tampa Bay's waterline tales of piracy have washed upon the shore over time, imbedding themselves in Tampa's lore.

As a child growing up in Tampa, I can recall more than one Halloween where I was excitedly dressed as a pirate. Truth be told, the costume retained a life for several days, if not weeks after the trick-or-treating was over. With a black pirate hat, a visually suppressing eye patch and a plastic sword hanging from my hip, I searched for buried treasure beneath the ground in my backyard. Much to my father's dismay, my digging exposed dirt and roots rather than gold and silver.

Thanks to cinematic movies, the life of a pirate during the eighteenth and nineteenth centuries appeared generally carefree, fun and lucrative. One simply needed to procure a seaworthy ship, a map guiding you to buried treasure, a cast of loyal-ish mates and of course, lots and lots of rum. As tales were passed down from generation to generation, details sometimes became sketchy. But the fate of the sea's scoundrels was always the same: defeat.

Such was the case with pirate, Pierre Leblanc. At one time, the waters along the coast of western Florida were under the scourge of pirate and privateer, Jean LaFitte. Known as a dangerous pirate and nothing short of a terror to society, he hid massive amounts of precious gold and jewels along the coast, most notably on Treasure Island. LaFitte charged Pierre LeBlanc with the task of protecting this fortune and equipped him with a palomino horse. Day after day, LeBlanc rode his horse along the coastline. The steed's gold coat shimmering under the Florida sun contrasted with its white mane and tail as they guarded LaFitte's buried treasure. As the story goes, a stranger happened upon the shores of Treasure Island. Confronted by LeBlanc, the stranger explained that he was simply hunting for snakes to sell their skins. Perhaps needing a break from isolation, the stranger and LeBlanc befriended one another. However, it would be a short-lived friendship.

After an evening of drinking together, the stranger found LeBlanc laying on top of one of LaFitte's treasure chest. The stranger took advantage of the situation and after a short brawl, beheaded LeBlanc and left the island with LaFitte's precious gold and jewels.

To this day, reports of a headless man riding a gold horse up and down the coast of Treasure Island are reported. Does LeBlanc's ghost, guilty of losing LaFitte's treasure, still guard unclaimed gold and jewels that remain buried under the sand? If you find yourself face to face with LeBlanc's ghost while walking the shoreline and you're brave enough, you can ask him.

Of course, the most popular and commercialized pirate name in the Tampa Bay area is Jose Gaspar, the ghost pirate, "Gasparilla". Gaspar's story paints him as a Spanish pirate that pillaged ships for their valuables along the coast of Florida. Gaspar and his men were greedy and relentless, overloading their ship with stolen jewels only to hide them on an island in the Gulf of Mexico, known as Gasparilla Island. Gaspar's eventual demise occurred during his final pillage of a merchant ship. Unbeknownst to Gaspar, the target was only disguised as a merchant ship. The ship was manned and gunned with enough power to finally take down the legendary pirate. Gaspar, refusing to be captured, wrapped an anchor chain around himself and threw himself down into the water. He would allow the sea to take his life but not another man. Like many pirate stories, his treasure is believed to be buried beneath the sands of Gasparilla Island, waiting for one lucky beachgoer to discover it.

Gaspar's legend inspired an annual celebration in Tampa that pays homage to an 1821 battle between Gaspar and opposing American forces in Tampa Bay. Thousands of spectators scream and cheer as a parade rolls and marches along Bayshore Boulevard, ending at Cass Street and Ashley Drive. Onlookers beg and plead for treasure to be thrown to them in the form of plastic bead necklaces and gold coins. Usually held in late January, the weather in Tampa Bay is nothing short of perfect and the spirit of Jose Gaspar penetrates the city.

Despite the widespread celebration of Gaspar's legend, many historians claim that he was a fabrication intended to boost the real estate market in the Tampa Bay area. But there are those that believe he was very real and still haunts the waters off Tampa Bay. Lore says that if you find yourself staring into the waters, on certain clear nights, you can see the head of Jose Gaspar, his hair a mess of seaweed, rising up from the water that claimed his body and life. But beware, for he will try to drag you down with him, deep into the water.

Off the water, pirates play another role and game for that matter in the Tampa Bay area. Our professional football team is named, the Tampa Bay Buccaneers. Home games are played at Raymond James Stadium which houses a massive pirate ship that sounds the shots of cannons to celebrate a Buccaneer score.

Plant Hall-The University of Tampa

Chapter Eight
Hotel Ghosts

Over the years, I've written much about my paranormal and metaphysical experiences. They are chronicled in The Dead: A True Paranormal Story and I've orally recounted them on podcasts as well as radio and television shows. While I do not claim to be an expert, I am certainly a person who has had a sizeable share of other-worldly experiences. And while I've seen, heard, sensed and felt things I cannot outright explain as normal activity in the physical world, I still maintain a left-brained, analytical filter to help define the events that unfold around me. For me, removing all possible explanations for a potentially paranormal experience makes the final determination of other-worldly activity that much richer.

Still, even events that seem to originate outside of our physical world have a reason behind their occurrence. We would be remiss to not anticipate that which can't often be seen or heard, especially if they possess the ability to harm us. Like people, ghosts, spirits and entities possess both good and bad intentions. I'm not suggesting that danger exists around every dark corner of a haunted location but with regard to the paranormal, my personal experience proves that it's more than prudent to beware of what lurks in the darkness.

Paranormal investigators around the globe painstakingly collect recordings, both visual and auditory to help them uncover the reasons behind a haunting. They spend hours and sometimes days listening to EVP's (Electronic Voice Phenomenon) in hopes of hearing a name, date or if they're really lucky, a ghost's true intention toward the living. For me, it's the latter that grabs my interest.

In my discussions I've encountered many people that felt a need to believe that there is some kind of existence for our spirit, or essence after our physical body ceases to function. Perhaps it's because life throws so much at us that knowing there's something beyond the struggle and suffering makes it worth the battle. Maybe it's the chance to reincarnate and not only see those we loved in this lifetime again but work to improve the kind of human being we were. Of course, finding out that life was more than just work, sleep and Netflix as we stand in line for entry through the pearly gates of Heaven surely makes the seventy-five years or so time well spent. Then again, there is a chance that once we pass, that's it and we wholly cease to exist.

Regardless of our particular beliefs and ultimate next stop on life's bus, there's a plethora of evidence to deduce that some spirits linger behind and haunt a specific location.

For several years I travelled extensively for work. If I had one complaint, it was the deep discomfort I felt while sleeping in an unfamiliar hotel room. In my experience, paranormal activity was more active in a hotel room, than any other public place that I spent an extended amount of time. I can't count the number of times I felt a touch on my shoulder or arm as I tried to sleep only to turn and find no one else in my room. One night, I woke up to the sound of a full water bottle falling to the floor. I tried to rationalize that it simply tipped over but I had placed it toward the back of the small dresser with several objects in front it which would have prevented it from rolling off. On another occasion I awoke to the bathroom light shining into the room. Confident that I had turned it off before going to sleep, I cautiously got up and checked the room for an intruder. Finding no one else in the room with me, I once again turned it off the bathroom light. Before I could walk the ten steps back to my bed, the bathroom light turned back on.

Have you ever stood in a lobby at three o'clock in the morning, shirtless and wearing only sleeping pants, to change hotel rooms? I have.

For another perspective, I asked best-selling author and paranormal investigator Joni Mayhan why hotel rooms are often the scene of paranormal activity.

"Many hotels are haunted due to their proximity to large highways which account for some of the entities due to accidents. But there are often other reasons for the hauntings.

They are frequently the site of suicides. Someone who premeditates their suicide might choose to perform the deed away from their family and friends. This way, the hotel maid will find their bodies instead of their family members.

At the moment of death, realization kicks in and they refuse to cross over into the light for fear they will end up in Hell instead of Heaven. In this case, they become earthbound ghosts, remaining at their place of death until they come to peace with their decision or are crossed over by a psychic medium."

While researching stories for this book, it was no surprise to learn that the building known as Plant Hall at The University of Tampa has reported accounts of paranormal activity since it was originally built and operated as a large hotel.

Built by railroad tycoon, Henry Plant in 1891, the former Tampa Bay Hotel accommodated hundreds of travelers including the likes of baseball legend, Babe Ruth and even Theodore Roosevelt.

Today, reports of apparitions in the science wing describe women dressed as servants appear and then disappear. Tanya, a student who had never seen a ghost before, described her incredible experience.

"I was sitting by myself very early one morning. I dropped my pen but before I could pick it up a woman appeared out of nowhere. She looked at me and pointed at the pen on the floor. I leaned down to pick it up and when I looked around she was gone. I swore she was there! I think she may have been a maid from when this was a hotel."

Tanya isn't the only one to experience the presence of servants. There are numerous reports of different voices conversing with one another with no physical person attached.

Those keen to the sound may also hear the rolling of dice, with no casino table in sight.

A few lucky visitors have seen a double apparition of a couple dancing in the former ballroom. A short-haired handsome man steps in time with his female partner. Her long hair swings behind her as she lovingly gazes into his eyes, enjoying a literally endless dance celebrating their love.

Other students report doors opening, footsteps and even the sound of someone sitting down near them, only to turn and find no one in the room with them.

Several students have reported seeing the ghost of a janitor. He's described as tall and wearing overalls while pushing a cleaning cart through the hallways. The thud of his work boots sound out in a heavy tone. How many tens of thousands of steps has he taken while both alive and dead?

The most famous and often seen apparition has become known as "The Brown Man". His nickname is derived from the brown suit he dons beneath long, white hair. Unlike the busy janitor who seems intent on pushing his cart, "The Brown Man" stares at you with glowing red eyes, as if taunting you. But don't stare back. It's been said that if you acknowledge his presence, he'll swiftly move toward you and confront you face to face and then suddenly disappear.

Are the ghosts of the former servants and janitor still working and dedicated, even in death? Is "The Brown Man" the ghost of Henry Plant himself, remaining behind to watch over his building? Maybe on your next visit, you'll be lucky enough to see one of them and ask them yourself.

Old Federal Courthouse

Chapter Nine
The White Shadow

Fueled by the temperance movement, it was believed that alcohol was responsible for the nation's crime, violence and poverty problems in the early twentieth century. Thus, in 1919 the Prohibition Act was enacted and began a sixteen-year run. While some of the country was likely compliant, the city of Tampa saw the law as more of a suggestion than a mandate. Thanks to widespread non-compliance by smugglers, bootleggers and local moonshiners, Tampa became known as one of the "wettest" cities with extreme alcoholic availability.

With the coastline's natural water inlets offering multiple avenues of delivery into Tampa, criminal activity grew at an alarming rate, including organized crime.

Tampa's first major crime boss and "Dean of the Underworld" was Charlie Wall. To the Latin population in the city he was referred to as "The White Shadow". Hardly the patron saint of morality, Wall profited immensely from countless brothels, speakeasies and illegal gambling sites throughout the city.

Wall enjoyed his underground reign until the Italian mafia took over. By the 1940's, Wall was almost completely retired out of the scene.

He resurfaced in 1950 but seemingly on the other side of crime. He was called to testify before a federal committee who had been investigating organized crime. Wall testified to the Kefauver committee in great detail everything he knew of the organized crime presence in Tampa.

As time passed, there were reported attempts of murder on Wall. Finally, one night in April of 1955, Wall's actions finally caught up with him.

According to the investigation, Wall was out drinking at one of his favorite spots. When it came time to go home, he was offered a ride by his friend, Nick Scaglione. The next time Wall was seen, he was barely recognizable.

Wall was found dead in his home, having been beaten with a wooden bat, stabbed ten times and his throat slit from ear to ear. Next to his bloody corpse sat the reason for his brutal murder: a copy of his testimony.

Scaglione was questioned and explained that he took Wall to his home and immediately left. He produced an airtight alibi for his whereabouts and was never charged in Wall's murder.

Over the years, Wall's apparition has been seen on the century-old federal courthouse's steps leading up to the building where he had testified. Some say he is pondering his actions, wishing he had never testified and endured such a brutal death.

Today, the courthouse has been converted to a triple-A, 4-Diamond 130-room hotel called the Le Meridien Hotel.

Britton Theatre

Chapter Ten
South Tampa Memories

My father was born in Alma, Michigan and my mother in Attleboro, Massachusetts. During the mid-1960's they moved to Florida with their newborn son, my older brother. They purchased a perfect first home in the Palma Ceia area of South Tampa in which to raise a family. Built in 1951, it occupied a corner lot with a spacious backyard, wrapping around the back of the house. In January of 1969, I became their second child, providing my brother with younger sibling. A year and a half later, we welcomed a third brother and completed our family.

Three growing boys soon necessitated the purchase of a larger home and in the early 1980's we moved to the Twelve Oaks subdivision in Town-n-Country. At the time it was the latest and greatest in Tampa's ever-expanding suburbia. Even at a young age I noticed the differences between the two homes.

Gone was the crushed seashell path of our South Tampa home as my parent's cars sat parked on a newly poured grey cement driveway. While I had grown accustomed to the crunch of shells beneath my feet, the basketball most assuredly now bounced to its full potential on the hard surface of cement.

Luckily, I was already tall enough to reach the thermostat that controlled the central heating and cooling system of our new home. It replaced the window air-conditioning unit and free-standing heater of our old home that my brothers and I had at times huddled around for quick relief from the extreme Florida weather.

The most exciting difference was the space and acquisition of our own bedrooms. We moved our boxes into a two-story, four bedroom, two and a half bathroom house that, to a child, seemed like a mansion compared to the two bedroom, one bathroom, single story home we had just left.

It was only later that I truly appreciated the charm and nostalgia of our South Tampa home and despite moving north, I still retain happy, vivid memories of my time south of Kennedy Blvd.

Unaware that my true calling was to play soccer, I spent a season playing baseball in the Palma Ceia Little League. I recall being nothing short of awful and my coach only placing me in the outfield for an inning or two to appease my attending parents in the bleachers. The final score of the game meant little to me compared to the event that followed the ninth inning: a hamburger, fries and a Coke at Pop n' Son's Diner. They sponsored our team and provided us with a celebratory meal, win or loss.

Located on the Interbay Peninsula and surrounded by Tampa Bay on the west, our proximity to the water provided many weekend days out on our boat. My mother lathered enough sunscreen on my skin to frost a cake but my pale, Scottish skin was certainly thankful for the protection against the intense Florida sun. I remember watching bobbers dance on the top of the water and gasping as an unseen fish pulled it beneath the surface. A helpful hand from my father ensured a winning battle against the unseen force at the other end of the fishing line and allowed me to smile proudly at the prize fish pulled into the boat.

Truly, one of my fondest memories takes place inside our old South Tampa home. We boasted what we call a Florida Room and most other states call a sunroom. Essentially, it's a room with two to three walls of windows or glass that allow the bright light of the sun to enter. Each December, we set up our Christmas tree in our Florida Room. My brothers and I would sit for hours watching the magical colored lights blink on and off opposite each other. We soaked in the smell of pine and the bright shiny tinsel, anxious for the inevitable day to arrive. Each day in the month saw another black "X" on the wall calendar, counting down the days until Santa arrived.

Finally, on Christmas morning, we woke to the smell of pies baking in the oven. The aromas of pumpkin, blueberry, cherry, apple and my personal favorite, lemon meringue wafted throughout the house as we stood in amazement at the bounty Santa had delivered. Dozens of presents filled our Florida room forcing us to step carefully to make our way to our stockings. Our tradition was for one of us to open one gift at a time, acknowledge it and then watch the next person open a gift, and so on. My memory times the process at well over one amazing, blissful hour.

Although both of my parents worked, we did many things together as a family. While I'm sure they would have enjoyed a restful day at home on their day off, they often saw to our entertainment. For me, going to the movies as a child was almost as exciting as going to Disney World.

The memory of seeing Superman with Christopher Reeves on the big screen is still very much alive in my mind. Not surprisingly, it sparked a love of superheroes and the beginning of a beloved collection of comic books.

The Britton Theatre first opened on August 15, 1956 as a single screen theatre that sat twenty-two hundred people. Designed by architect James E. Casale, it held its own for over a decade until it was forced to redesign and accommodate the increasing number of movies being made. Closed during renovation, the theater reopened in 1973 with a three-screen offering.

While the theatre has its place of significance in the history of Tampa, it surprises some people that it has been reported as haunted. However, their shock doesn't stem from their disbelief in the occurrence of the paranormal. In fact, their acceptance of other-worldly events is what fuels their confusion.

As far as anyone questioned knows, no one has passed away inside the theatre and there aren't any reports of dark, tragic events. Despite the absence of what might be considered a reason for a haunting, strange and unexplainable experiences have been reported.

An apparition is defined as the supernatural appearance of a person or thing, especially a ghost. Certainly the experience of seeing an apparition is one of the most terrifying things that can happen to a person, particularly if you are alone. For several visitors and workers of the Britton Theatre, this has been a frightening reality.

An employee was working late when she caught an image out of the corner of her eye. Turning quickly, she froze as an image of a woman formed on the balcony in front of her. The apparition's face was emotionless and stoic. The employee gasped, rubbed her eyes and suddenly the image of the ghostly woman had vanished.

Several reports of supernatural movement come from both employees and visitors. According to several woman, doors in the ladies will close and lock by themselves. As if an invisible woman is there for the same reason as those that are alive, the doors reopen and the toilets flush on their own.

The reports of paranormal activity have yet to be linked to any particular person or event. They do seem to be more prevalent and understandably scary late at night.

Wesley found himself working late with one other worker. Standing side by side, he heard a voice. Turning to his coworker, he asked him what he said, to which he replied. "I didn't say anything."

Again, Wesley heard a voice in the near distance. He once again turned to his coworker who immediately answered his unspoken yet obvious query, "Yeah, I heard that too."

They stood quiet for another minute, straining their ears to hear. What happened next sent Wesley running out of the theatre.

"As I stood there, listening for the voice I felt a cold presence against my cheek. In the same moment, I heard someone say my name, right into my ear. But, not only did I hear my name being spoken, I felt breathe in my ear."

Wesley ran as fast as he could out of the theatre and to his car, never looking back.

Today, the small theatre still operates in South Tampa's Britton Plaza. Although it may only offer a couple of movies and times, keep your eyes and ears open for it could give you a terrifying experience you'll never forget.

The Sulphur Springs Water Tower

Chapter Eleven
Fact, Legend and Lore

I can truly call only one city my home. Tampa is where I was born and raised, played sports, went to school and the prom. It's where I currently work and reside and celebrate every holiday. And, for the better part of my residence I've been driving along the streets and highways of Tampa. However, it's only in recent years that I realized how much I still didn't know about my city.

As many of you know, owning a home in Tampa with a guest room allows us to provide hospitality and even guided tours of our city. Friends and family can visit Busch Gardens, Adventure Island and Ybor City. Across the bridge to St. Petersburg they can visit the extraordinary Salvador Dali Museum and of course, take a ride across I-4 to the visit the Disney and Universal theme parks.

One day while driving along I-275, one of my visiting passengers pointed to a landmark and asked me what it was.

"That's the Sulphur Springs Tower." I replied in a knowing tone that suggested I had somehow built it many years ago.

"What's its history?"

My voice fell to a clearly unconfident tone and I delivered a vague response that would be severely undersold. "It...provided water...to people."

So much for being nominated for the *Ambassador to Tampa* position.

As is often the case with history, there are records of documented facts and sometimes a much less documented mix of legend and lore. In the case of the Sulphur Springs Tower, its story has all three of these elements.

Standing two-hundred and fourteen feet tall, the tower was built in 1927 and served to provide water to the Sulphur Springs Hotel and Mave's Arcade, Florida's first mall.

The Sulphur Springs Hotel was a resort and recreation facility that boasted adjacency to the healing properties of the mineral waters in the Hillsborough River. The hotel was famous for its stunning first and second floor classical style front arcade. For years it thrived as a destination resort for those with the means. Later, it struggled during the Great Depression's suffering economy. Business took another hit as flooding waters challenged operations to say the least. The resort changed hands over the years and its time seemed over when its pool became a public swimming facility. Finally, after closing for good in 1975, the building was demolished in 1976.

The water tower weathered the years and even inspired the Tower drive-in theatre that opened in 1951. It remained operational through the 1960's until water was supplied by the city of Tampa. Ultimately, the tower was decommissioned in 1971.

In 1989 it was declared a historic landmark but wasn't safe from vandalism and decay. Thankfully, in 2005 it was purchased by the city of Tampa which literally and figuratively cemented its place and protection in Tampa's history.

Some speak of a time when the tower was used as a lighthouse to help guide mariners and warn against pirates as they made their way to land. That story fails to gain altitude since the tower was constructed by Grover Poole in 1927. However, given Tampa's pirate presence in the past, one could see how that lore could have been created.

Legend has it that during the difficult economic strife of The Great Depression, some distraught individuals used the tower to end their suffering. Losing their battle with depression after having lost all of their worldly possessions including their homes, they climbed to the top, threw themselves off the side of the tower and plunged to their death.

I spoke with Matt who has also lived his whole life in the Tampa Bay area and he shared a story about the night he visited the tower and why he has never been back.

"When I was sixteen and was getting ready to go out on a date with my girlfriend. I heard that the old tower in Sulphur Springs was supposed to be haunted, so I thought it would be fun to take her there. At first she didn't want to go but I finally convinced her. We got there a little after ten o'clock. It was dark but we brought flashlights. I wasn't sure what I expected to see but it didn't take long for us to turn around and leave."

Matt paused while recalling that night. His hands rubbed together nervously in his lap.

"We walked to the tower through the nighttime darkness except for our flashlights. As I was walking my foot hit something hard and I tripped over whatever was on the ground. It felt like I kicked a bag of rocks. Immediately I shined my flashlight on the ground but there was nothing there. I looked all over but there was nothing that I could have tripped over. It was just flat ground. Then, we heard a loud scream. It kept getting louder and louder as if someone was running toward us. I looked all around us but I didn't see anyone. My girlfriend suddenly started screaming. I looked over and she had her flashlight pointed to the sky. I looked up and saw a body falling through the air. It landed with a thud exactly where I had been tripped. My girlfriend wouldn't stop screaming and started to run back to the car. I followed her for a few feet and then turned back around. I couldn't believe my eyes: the body was gone. I looked all over for the body, or anyone for that matter but didn't find anything. There wasn't even an imprint where the body had landed to prove that it was even there. Needless to say, we never went back."

There are many reports of people being seen throwing themselves off the top of the tower and disappearing upon hitting the ground. Some believe the traumatic event of suicide could have left a recording in the spiritual energy atop the tower that continually replays itself. Others theorize that perhaps the spirits that took their lives are confused. They are trapped in a futile cycle of trying to kill themselves, not realizing they are already dead.

If you visit the Sulphur Springs Tower and see one of these disembodied souls, send them love and light and say a prayer in hopes that they find soon find peace.

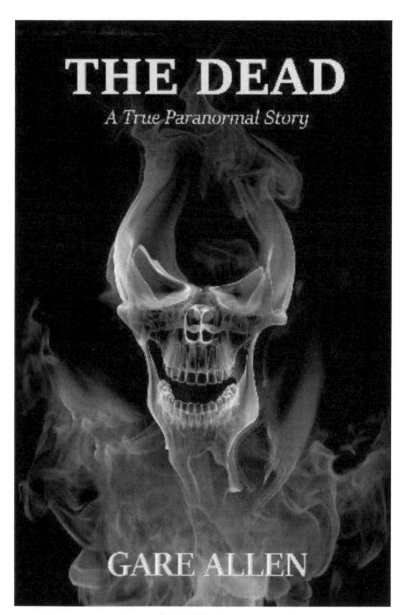

THE DEAD

A True Paranormal Story

GARE ALLEN

The Dead book cover

Chapter Twelve
The Dead

As you might have guessed, I have an interest in the paranormal and metaphysical world. Throughout my life I have had many experiences, some I welcomed and some not so much. I chronicled my experiences from the age of twelve until adulthood in a book called *The Dead*. Below is an excerpt detailing the events of my life after purchasing a home in North Tampa that I would soon discover to be haunted.

It was the summer of 1999 and after years of renting, I was looking to buy a house.

The realtor received my requirements of a home with three bedrooms, two bathrooms, a pool and a selling price of less than one hundred thousand dollars.

She ran a search through her listings and suggested a subdivision that I had actually lived in for a year after my parent's divorce. Hardly fond of the area, I declined even considering a house in that neighborhood. However, after a few unsuccessful months of house hunting, she circled back to my black-listed subdivision and I gave in.

It was the beginning of September when I looked at a house that met all of my criteria and even boasted a lake view.

The house was owned by a woman who had moved to Maryland. During a recent separation and pending divorce from her husband, he had died and she was selling it, "as is". While the structure of the home appeared solid, the walls were in need of paint, the carpets were soiled and the pool water was a dark green. The unclear water concerned me as it hid any potential damage to the pool itself and may have been in need of costly repair.

I soon discovered that the house had been sitting empty and clearly ignored for several months, which was the apparent cause of its desperate need of cleaning.

One thing in particular that disturbed me was that the front bedroom carpet was so badly stained that it was almost completely black. I recall wondering if someone had spilled motor oil.

I had planned on replacing the carpet anyway, so I made an offer for exactly the price that she was asking. As long as the house passed the structural inspection and the pool didn't leak, it would still be a great deal.

Within a few days, the owner countered with a significantly increased price and cited that there had been "heavy interest in the house." Apparently she felt she could get more than her original asking price.

No thanks.

Over the next three weeks, the continued house-hunt yielded nothing of interest. Then, the seller's realtor called and asked if I was still interested. I decided to see the house again.

To my delight, the walls had been freshly painted, the carpets had been replaced and the pool was crystal clear. I submitted an offer that was much lower than the inflated price with which she had countered. My offer was even slightly lower than my original bid and it was accepted.

The closing on the house occurred late in October and I moved in during the Halloween weekend, despite my initial blockade.

"Buyers are liars." The realtor joked and then stated that her intention was *not* to be crass.

It sounded crass.

A few days prior to the move, I enlisted the support of my friend, Carl to assist with some minor work. We needed to install new window blinds, closet shelves, ceiling fans and bathroom mirrors.

For some reason, the bathroom mirrors were missing.

Needing additional supplies, I left him at the house and drove to the local Home Depot. When I returned, I found him lying flat on the carpet in the living room and engaged in conversation. He was more than startled when he saw me walk through the front door.

Carl suffered from a bad back. According to him, he was hurting from being on the ladder all morning, so he had laid down on the carpet to stretch out his back.

He then claims he heard me and assumed that I had returned from the hardware store. He began a dialogue with a voice that responded to him from the front bedroom.

"Gare, I'm taking a break. My back is killing me."

A voice asked. "What are you working on?"

Carl replied, "Hanging new blinds over the sliding glass doors."

"What was wrong with the old ones?" asked the voice.

Carl laughed. "I don't know. I guess you like to spend money."

Just then I appeared through the front door. Carl turned his head and could not reconcile that I had just then returned.

"Where were you?" Carl asked, startled and confused.

I carried in bags of screws and other needed items. "I told you, Home Depot."

Carl slowly and painfully sat up and looked down the hallway at the front bedroom. "Then, who have I been talking to?"

Carl relayed his short conversation with the voice and the hairs on the back of my neck stood up. More than curious, he got up and we both walked, slowly, to the front bedroom, only to find it empty.

Confused and finding no explanation, we returned to work. Then, Carl realized that his hammer was no longer on his tool belt. With the exception of our tools, the shelves and ceiling fans, the house was empty. We had not moved in any boxes, furniture, household items, etc. He had been using his hammer in the same room in which we stood just minutes prior to me coming back from the hardware store. We searched the entire, empty house. It had vanished and, to this day, we have not found it.

During lunch, we ate in the backyard to enjoy the view of the small lake. The landscaping was sparse, but the yard boasted eight giant, lush queen palms. As I surveyed the lot, I imagined the tropical green, yellow and red foliage I would plant. Soon, a colorful landscape would replace the unsightly, grey dirt.

My eyes caught a glimpse of something white on the ground. I walked over to see a display both haunting and disturbing and immediately called a metaphysical spiritualist and psychic, Dane.

I described my find to Dane on my cell phone as I stood over an unsettling sight.

"There are dozens of white and grey bird feathers placed flat on the ground. They're arranged like a fan, but a full 360 degrees." Being an animal lover, I felt a tinge of sadness as I continued the description. "In the center, oh my God, it's a beak of a small bird."

Dane remained unemotional despite my growing discomfort. "What else?"

I continued. "The sharp ends of the feathers are all pointing to the tiny mouth. In each corner around the feathers are four small, white rocks." I became agitated along with a sense of trepidation as the parts of a dead bird stared back at me. "What the hell is this?"

Dane's voice was now heavy with concern. "How long has it been there?"

"I don't know. I just noticed it today." I replied, frustrated and trying to determine a timeframe.

We had walked the entire lot the day of closing and had stood just a few feet from where the feathers were. Surely, we would have seen it then if it had been there. In all honesty, I couldn't be sure.

I asked him repeatedly to explain what he thought it was, but he refused. Instead, he urged me to obtain sea salt and cover the area with it.

While I assumed that this was some kind of ritualistic display, I had never seen one before, let alone on my property. There was a strange and terrifying sense of a personal attack or warning surrounding the find. Which is odd since the house sat vacant for over four months and the one surviving owner didn't even care enough to return and oversee the sale. Who would have any interest in the house now and what would they have against me?

I returned the next day with sea salt and soon the display of bird feathers turned into a white mound of a cleansing condiment. Despite my research, I could not find any reference to a ritualistic display similar to what I had found.

I moved in on the following Saturday, which happened to be the day before Halloween. Capitalizing on the opportunity to deter any future vandalism, I bought only brand name candy bars to win over the neighborhood kids.

I was basically bribing them to *not* egg my house.

My buddy, Dirk, was helping me unload the truck when a group of children rode their bicycles up the driveway and stopped just outside the garage.

Apparently, the unloading of boxes and furniture out of a moving truck didn't paint a clear enough picture as one of the young boys asked, "Are you moving in?"

I don't dislike conversations with children. But, I prefer to have them with bright children.

"Uh, yeah." I delivered, somewhat facetiously, while I motioned my rolling eyes to the moving truck.

"Do you know the history of the house?" the boy asked. His follow-up question would not receive my rolling eyes of dismissal, this time. In fact, his far-too-eager tone suggested he had at least a little bit on intel that might be of interest to me.

Cautiously, I replied, "No."

Without hesitation and with way too much enthusiasm, he blurted, "It's haunted!"

Dirk burst into laughter. "You bought the Amityville House!"

Great, now I had to address two children.

I leered at Dirk. "Really?"

I walked up to the young boy, who was visibly trembling while trying to contain his excitement. Fearing he might pee in his pants, I quickly asked, "Ok, what happened here?"

The little kid took center stage as he leaned back on his bike and folded his arms in front of him. The other children stared at him expectantly. I imagined that they had all heard his story at least once before but their eyes were wide with anticipation as he told us of his first-hand experience.

"The man that lived here killed himself and I found him!"

A suicide in the home that I had just purchased was definitely not what I was expecting him to say. I assumed that he had seen a ghost in the window or maybe the lights flickered on and off late at night inside a known-empty house. Certainly, I never imagined that he would proclaim that he had found a dead body.

Out of the corner of my eye, I saw Dirk take a few steps closer so he could hear the child better.

The boy looked to the wall of the garage to his left. "He shot himself in the front bedroom. There's the bullet hole."

I tilted my head and narrowed my eyes as belief began to root itself inside my mind. After walking over to the garage wall I noted that the hole was located on the drywall, just above my waistline. The opposite, interior wall was, indeed, in the front bedroom.

As if a class bell had rung, the group of children abruptly left. Without uttering a word, Dirk and I went inside the house and headed straight for the bedroom.

I ran my finger along the drywall near the height of my waistline. It wasn't long before I found a cold, round pocket of undried putty. I pushed my finger into it with ease. My friend remained quiet and left the room in favor of resuming the unpacking of the truck. As I followed behind him, I recalled the severely stained carpet that had been replaced by the time of my second visit. It was clear that those permeating, dark stains had been blood.

The young, neighborhood informant returned to my house the next night in costume and in search of Halloween candy. He was accompanied by his mother, who introduced herself as my next door neighbor.

A few days later, I arrived home as she was working in her yard. I seized the opportunity to get the backstory on the incident. At first, the subject matter was uncomfortable for her and she was reluctant to discuss it. But, in the end, she felt that I, as the new owner, deserved to know.

Or, I was overbearing and she felt that if she told me what I wanted to know, I would cease my relentless questioning.

Yeah, that sounds more likely.

She told me that a childless couple had owned the house prior to my purchase.

In respect of their privacy, I'll refer to them as Rick and Carol in lieu of using their real names.

The story goes that Carol, who the neighbors had generally considered to be crazy, left Rick and filed for divorce.

Carol was known to be emotionally unstable and even abusive at times. Neighbors described her taking morning walks up and down the street in her bath robe while chastising anyone in her path for their glares of judgment. I also heard that she had a soft spot for stray cats. This was easily confirmed when I often woke to countless feral felines huddled in my backyard awaiting food.

Rick became depressed and his behavior suggested that he was also losing a little of his own sanity.

Shortly after Carol's departure, Rick began approaching the neighbors and offering them his furniture and personal belongings. He told them that he would rather they have it than allow the lawyers to take it all from him. One neighbor claims that Rick told him that he had flushed ten thousand dollars down the toilet in an effort to keep his wealth from the attorneys.

I heard this story more than once. In one version, the money had been given away and in another, he hid it in the walls of the house.

Despite my inclination to put a hammer to the drywall, I never looked.

Rick held a part time job at a department store and worked every Tuesday and Thursday. He claimed it was "something to do".

The remainder of his time was spent lamenting, to anyone who would listen, about his impending divorce and how he cared for his dog; a giant breed mix of a Great Pyrenees and a Golden Retriever.

Rick was also known to help the neighborhood children with their bicycle repairs. For all intents and purposes he was considered to be a nice, albeit distraught, guy.

Rick was unusually home one Thursday morning and retrieving something from the trunk of his car when one of the neighbors saw him. When asked why he wasn't at work, he explained that he had a dentist appointment. According to the neighbor, that was the last time Rick was seen alive.

Two days later, the young boy from next door required assistance with his bike. Rick's car was in the driveway so he proceeded to his front door. Surprised to find an open door, the child rang the doorbell and called out to Rick, but he only heard the barks of Rick's dog from the backyard. When Rick didn't appear after the boy's follow-up knock, he decided to enter the house.

He stood at the end of the long hallway that led to the front bedroom with his mouth agape as he witnessed a gruesome scene.

Rick's lifeless body was sprawled across the blood stained carpet. The walls were washed red while bits and pieces of his head peppered a ten food radius. A gun rested in his lap; the obvious cause of the tragic death.

Terrified, the boy ran to get his mother. She returned to behold the same horrific atrocity and immediately called the authorities.

Later, my neighbor would recall the small table, to the right of Rick's body and in front of the small closet. It held several burning candles and multiple pictures of his estranged wife. She described it as a shrine that was adorned with many strange objects including chicken's feet, tiny homemade dolls, and small bags tied with twine. In the center of the display was a handwritten note that read, "Carol, you win."

Suddenly, the dead bird offering in my backyard appeared to have some relevance.

I called Dane and explained the home's recent sad and disturbing history. He walked me through the process of "cleaning" a house. That is, a spiritual and energy cleansing, using salt, sage, white candles and lemons.

After lighting the end of a sage smudge wand I moved through my house. Committed to reach every corner, nook and cranny with the heavy scent of sage, I opened closet doors, shower curtains and even cabinets. Next, I moved through my home holding a white candle. While rotating it in front of me, I envisioned the residual negativity being sucked into the candle and shot up and out to the ethers where it would dissipate. The glass surrounding the candle warmed in my hand and soon the temperature in the house increased five to six degrees.

I applied salt to every window sill and doorway, both inside and outside my home. As I followed Dane's instructions I recalled a particular channeling session in which his spirit guide explained the necessity of continuous cleansing.

"Think of negativity as insects and bugs that find their way into homes in search of food and living space."

Watching someone channel a spirit can be unnerving. Especially when a woman's speaks from a man's mouth. Dane's head swiveled back and forth in an even movement. His eyes remained closed but the lids fluttered as if trying to pry themselves open. The woman's voice boomed from his mouth as she enunciated every other syllable.

"You use chemicals to chase away the unwanted pests and cleaning formulas to create an inhospitable environment. This is not dissimilar to the cleansing of a home of undesirable entities using sage, salt and holy water."

She paused and a pleased smile appeared on Dane's face. "Those pesky creatures return when the chemicals have dissipated, surely enticed by the dirty dishes left in the kitchen sink."

The smile on Dane's face was replaced with raised eyebrows as she continued. "To complete our analogy, the dark beings are lured to your living space by your negative moods and behavior. Indeed, contrary to popular belief, like attracts like."

Having recalled the session on cleansing, it made much more sense now that I was actually applying the practices with the sage, candle and salt.

Getting back to the task at hand, I placed half slices of lemons in each corner of the front bedroom for a period of seven days. A successful cleansing would produce black lemons as they would have absorbed all the negative energy. A week later, I found that the lemon's color remained unchanged.

Uh-oh.

After talking with Dane, he suggested I try again. I decided I would repeat the cleaning process the very next morning.

I was unaware that later that night, I would receive a message that whatever was in the house, was definitely still there.

After dinner that evening, I moved to my office and sat at my desk working, or rather, playing on the internet. To my right was a closed window that provided a view of the courtyard. Normally, at night, I kept the blinds closed for privacy and this evening was no exception. As usual, my faithful black Lab, Sobek, slept below the window, just a few feet away from me.

I was surfing the internet and felt like I was being watched. I grew more and more uncomfortable and was certain someone was standing next to me. I tried to shake off the fear when the window blinds made a startling noise. Stunned, I jumped out of my chair. It was as if someone had taken their hand and smacked them from right to left. After hearing the sound of the hit, I watched as the blinds swung back and forth and produced the scraping sound of their interaction. It occurred to me that my office is adjacent to the front bedroom. In fact, the closet in my office aligns with the closet in the bedroom.

Was there a correlation?

Sobek also reacted, which helped solidify my belief in the uncanny occurrence. If the dog also saw and/or heard it, it couldn't have been my imagination.

My agitated dog, jolted out of slumber, emitted a low growl and was on all fours while sniffing the air for an explanation. Eventually, the blinds slowed their movement and rested back into place.

To appease the rational left side of my brain, I reviewed the environmental particulars. Aside from the pups, I was home alone. The ceiling fan was off and the air conditioning had not yet kicked on to cool the house for the night. I was awake and alert and had not been drinking or taken any mind-altering substances.

It boils down to this. The blinds were moving after I heard them being hit. Something or someone did it because window treatments don't move by themselves. It wasn't me and it wasn't my sleepy Retriever. I am reminded of a borrowed quote I heard in a Star Trek movie:

"If you eliminate the impossible, whatever remains, however improbable, must be the truth."

Many would find it improbable that I agitated an unfriendly spirit when I performed a failed, cleansing process, but, not impossible.

Early the next morning, I attempted to clean the front bedroom and entire house once again. While I waited for the darkening of the lemon halves over the next week, I experienced some more unsettling activity.

For days, things went missing and were never to be found. Included in the list is a check, a set of keys, my driver's license, and even a new license plate for my truck.

I distinctly recall placing the plate on my desk. Later that day, I found the appropriate screwdriver but when I returned to retrieve the plate, it was no longer there. It was metal and measured around four by ten inches, yet it had vanished.

At the end of the seven day period, I found that the lemons were still quite yellow. I became frustrated and paced the front bedroom. It was cold, indeed, much colder than the rest of the house.

I've read that entities can basically suck the energy out of a room and even people. They may use the stolen energy to manipulate physical reality, such as taking keys and license plates, and even manifest themselves. The thought caused me to recall Dane's and his guide's agreement of her use of his physical body.

Dane would be overwhelmed with a positive energy after channeling his guide. It was easy for me to conclude that my moods and behavior could be easily affected by the particular entities that surround me. That gave me even more fervor to remove the negativity in my home.

I closed the air conditioning vent which redirected the cooled air to other parts of the house. My goal was to test my theory that if the room remained cold without air conditioning, something else was dropping the temperature.

The bedroom maintained a cold and heavy atmosphere for days afterward and I had my answer.

After another call to Dane, he agreed to come over the next day and tackle the negativity, himself.

I thanked him profusely, hung up and called the realtor who had listed the house. It seemed to me that there would be a clause, or even a law that required sellers to disclose the occurrences of a suicide or murder in a home on the market. I was half right. Full disclosure is required in some states, but not in good, old Florida.

Hiding behind the law, the realtor copped a slight attitude and asked me if it would have changed my decision to buy the home if I had known about the unfortunate event.

Without hesitation, I replied, "Probably not, but I would have offered less for it. And, morally, don't you think you should have told me?"

Not surprisingly, my direct question abruptly ended the conversation.

When Dane arrived to my house the next morning, I was surprised to see that he was beyond pissed off.

He told me that whoever or whatever was in the front bedroom, had gone to his apartment the night before and attacked him. Dane explained that he was relaxing on his couch and watching television when the room temperature dropped to, what felt like, freezing. He could see his breath in the frigid air when, suddenly, he felt pain run from the bottom of his feet to the top of his head. He writhed in agony for several seconds and heard a deep, sinister voice in his ear, telling him to "stay away." Then, the pain disappeared and the temperature in the room returned to normal.

What concerned Dane the most was that the entity had the ability to enter his apartment. He explained that he routinely performs rituals and protects his living space from any unwanted spirits, good or bad. This dark entity was disturbingly strong enough to break through his protective barriers and well aware of our intentions to banish it.

Dane had come prepared with a printed ritual that required our mutual participation. After hours of salting, smudging, chanting, and candle burning, we felt that we had succeeded in banishing the negative spirit.

The following morning at three o'clock, I woke up to see something that would prove that our banishing efforts had failed. I was unprepared for the unholy encounter that would haunt me for the rest of my life.

I opened my eyes to see a grossly burned demon staring coldly at me. Its face was hot red with burned folds of skin running from its forehead down to its neck. Piercing yellow eyes targeted a palpable hate at me. The demonic being was only inches from my face and reeked of sulfur.

The demon leaned over my bed with its claw-like hands on both sides of my body. I suddenly realized that I was paralyzed and unable to feel my limbs. Frightening panic engulfed my sense of being. Unable to access my voice, I strained, unsuccessfully, to speak. Inside my head, I cried out for help.

Unbelievably, the demon's expression reacted to my inner cries and pulled back. In the same instant, I sat up, screaming at the top of lungs for help. The demon disappeared. Sobek, who was at the foot of my bed, was jolted awake at my outburst. He looked up at me, confused.

Suddenly, our attention was pulled to the front of the house where we heard a "thud" from the front bedroom.

Understandably, it took a few minutes for me to gather the courage to investigate the sound.

Finally, I adopted a defensive posture at the intrusion into my bedroom. I grabbed a bat and jumped out of bed.

With a hardly effective weapon against a ghost in my hand, I walked toward the front bedroom only to be stopped at the beginning of the hallway. The obvious reason for the loud sound stared back at me as I found the door to the front bedroom closed.

My fear quickly became anger and I flung open the bedroom door. With a baseball bat on my shoulder and a "get the hell out of my house" expression, I peered into darkness. The room was empty. Despite the closed air conditioning vent, I felt its cold air seep out at me.

The next day, Dane was kind enough to attempt, one more time, a spirit removal. He arrived to my house armed with a ritual that included prayers and some kind of binding spell. I sat this one out, but he was successful in securing the entity to a small corner of the closet, with no access to the bedroom or the remainder of the house. His hope was that with restricted movement, it would leave to find a more hospitable environment.

It was better than nothing.

Over the years, there has been some minor activity such as missing objects and noises but nothing egregious. I did take notice that it was during house renovations that the harmless ghost parlor tricks of lost keys and knocks on the walls, would occur.

After a visit from an impartial, unknown psychic, my assumptions were confirmed. Yes, we bound the demon and it did not have access to the living space in the house, but, I still had at least, one ghost. It was a lost soul.

The psychic woman identified the ghost as Rick, the previous owner, who had committed suicide in the front bedroom.

She went on to explain that Rick had been using some sort of voodoo magic in an attempt to bring back his wife. Unfortunately, he inadvertently conjured a demon, which remained after his passing.

The clairvoyant tried to connect with Rick and show him the way to his light and help him cross over.

I truly hope Rick found peace.

Welcome to Seminole Heights Sign

Chapter Thirteen
The Mean Woman

After ten years of renting, Tucker and Alyssa had finally saved enough money to buy their first home together. The couple spent several weeks house-hunting but couldn't find the right house for them. Then one day, their realtor took them to see a house in the historic district of Seminole Heights.

Seminole Heights is one of the earliest residential areas in Tampa, dating back to the early twentieth century. The area struggled economically during the late part of the century but the residents worked together to elevate their neighborhood. Today the community and surrounding area is filled with charm, eclectic stores, trendy restaurants and several brew pubs. The area has three neighborhoods including Southeast Seminole Heights, South Seminole Heights and Old Seminole Heights.

Tucker and Alyssa smiled as they walked up to the house. As their realtor had hoped, the warm and welcoming front porch delivered a solid first impression. The charm of the overhanging eaves and low pitched-roof lines of the bungalow style home proudly boasted the classic architecture of almost one century ago. Once inside of the home, the open floor plan ignited excitement regarding décor and furniture placement. The one-story, two-bedroom home was smaller than the other homes they had seen, but the couple felt that it was the perfect size for their family. With the selling price exactly where they wanted it, they decided to purchase their first home.

When they first moved in, their daughters, Ashley and Brianna were eight and six years-old. They had always loved each other and were best friends.

But something changed and it almost destroyed Tucker and Alyssa's family. Here is her story.

There was a very strange, unsetting, confusing and just plain scary time just after they moved in when they didn't understand what was happening. And during this time, Tucker and Alyssa made some false assumptions that upset everyone in their family. They were all at odds with one another and it was tearing them apart.

For Brianna's birthday, her aunt gave her a collection of goofy socks. They were brightly colored with cartoon characters and had funny sayings on them. Brianna instantly loved them. She would wear a pair every day to show off to her friends and even wore them to bed. Her parents couldn't get them off of her to even wash them without a struggle.

One night she had gone to bed and Alyssa heard her saying, 'Stop it, stop doing that!' At first she ignored it because she assumed that their dog Brady was licking her or bothering her and she was just trying to get him to leave her alone so she could sleep. Brady could be a little protective where the girls were concerned and always slept in their room. Then, she heard her say it again. 'Stop it! Why are you doing that?' Just then she heard Brady growling from her bedroom. She didn't know what to think because Brady was always a sweet dog. Alyssa called Tucker and they ran to the girl's room. Tucker flew open the door and they just paused and took in what they saw while trying to make sense of it.

Brianna was sitting up in her bed. She had the covers off so they can see that she has only one of her socks on. For some reason, she's got her hands wrapped around her leg with the sock. Brady is staring at the end of her bed and letting out a low growl. His eyes are just staring straight ahead. They tried to get his attention but he was one hundred percent focused on something, although they had no idea what it was.

Tucker flipped on the light and just as he did, Brady relaxes, sees them and starts wagging his tail acting normal again.

They asked Brianna why she was telling Brady to 'Stop it!'

She said 'I wasn't, Mommy. I was talking to the mean woman, she wanted my socks.'

Tucker and Alyssa looked at each other and figured that she had just woken up from a bad dream. Ashley had been sleeping in her bed on the other side of the bedroom but rolled over and asked what was happening. They told her it was nothing and both girls fell back to sleep.

The next night, the same thing happened. They put the girls to bed and within thirty minutes, they heard Brianna saying 'Stop it!' over and over. As they made their way to the girl's room, they could hear Brady growling but it was louder and meaner than the night before, almost like he was going to attack someone or something. Alyssa and Tucked opened the door and saw pretty the much the same thing they did the night before. Except, Ashley was standing next to Brianna's bed.

Alyssa asked Ashley what she was doing and she just shrugged her shoulders and said, 'I was trying to help'.

Her mom then asked, 'Help with what?'

Before Ashley could answer, Brianna said, 'The mean woman wants my socks, Mommy.'

Then, the same thing happens that did the night before. Brady stops growling and starts wagging his tail and the girls fall back to sleep.

At first the couple thought that their daughter was having bad dreams but Brady's behavior really bothered them. What was he growling at?

The strange behavior continued the next night.

As usual, they put the girls to bed and soon after they heard Brianna saying, 'Leave me alone! Stop it!' Tucker and Alyssa go to the bedroom and he grabbed the handle and pushed on the door but it wouldn't open. There isn't a lock on the girl's bedroom door so unless something is blocking the door, there's no reason for it to not open.

Tucker stepped in front of his wife and tried to force the door open. While he's pushing and literally throwing his body against the bedroom door, they can hear Brady growling and it's even louder than the two previous nights. Something had him riled up and it was really scaring them at this point.

Alyssa was starting to panic and between Brianna's pleading, Brady's growling and Tucker cursing and running his shoulder into the door, it all finally got to her and she screamed as loud as she could, 'Open the door!'"

As if it had a power of its own, that door flew wide open. Tucker reaches his hand inside and flips on the light switch. As the light fills the room, Brady calms down, wags his tail and just walks away. Brianna is laying down on her bed and Ashley is at the foot of her bed with Brianna's legs in her hands.

Alyssa asked, 'What are you doing?'

She said, 'I'm trying to take off her socks. She's not supposed to wear them to bed!'

At this point Alyssa's fear turned to anger. She yelled, 'Leave your sister alone and let her sleep!'

They put the girls back to bed and started walking back to the living room when they heard Brianna scream. Tucker had a long day at work so she told him, 'I'll handle this, go relax.'

Alyssa admits that she was pretty angry and basically fed up. She didn't understand what the big deal was about her socks but thought maybe Ashley was jealous of the attention they brought her sister and she felt left out. She opened the girl's bedroom door and she finds both of them standing in front of the doorway. Brianna is holding her left cheek and crying.

Alyssa asked, 'What happened?'

Brianna said, 'She slapped me!'

She couldn't believe what she heard. Her girls had never fought. They always got along and even when they disagreed they certainly didn't slap each other.

She looked at Ashley and asked her, 'Did you slap your sister?'

She yelled back, 'No! The mean woman did it!'

Both girls were now crying and their mom is standing in front of them, stunned at the thought of Ashley striking her sister.

Alyssa took a breath and looked at Brianna. 'Who slapped you?'

Through her tears, she said, 'The mean woman.'

Becoming more and more frustrated she said, 'Brianna! Don't lie to me. Did your sister slap you?'

She screamed in response, 'No!'

Alyssa was beside herself and didn't know what to think. She took the girls to the kitchen and got them some water. Brianna's face was a little red so she put some ice in a washcloth and she held it on her cheek for a half an hour or so. They were all tired so she put them back to bed and they slept through the night.

The next morning she made the girls breakfast and asked them what had been going on. Brianna told her that an old woman appears in their room and tells her that it's not ladylike to wear socks to bed and tries to take them off. And when she refused to take them off last night, the old woman slapped her.

Alyssa asked Ashley why she was holding her sister's legs. She explained that she was trying to help her sister. She crossed my arms and just stared at her daughters. Part of her thought they were making it all up but another part of her believed them as they've always been good, honest kids.

Then Brianna said something that really freaked out her mom. She said, 'Brady saw her.'

Alyssa remembered Brady's behavior and asked, 'Is that why he was growling?'

Ashley replied, 'Yes. She doesn't like Brady. She said dogs are dirty.'

She had accused the girls of making up an invisible friend but they argued with her that the mean woman was real. In all honesty, she could have handled an imaginary friend but the thought of Ashley slapping her sister was something she couldn't wrap my head around. Unfortunately, Tucker felt that Ashley should be punished and that started a long run of arguments and their fighting only upset the girls more.

For weeks, Brianna came out of her room crying from being slapped. Tucker punished Ashley each time and Alyssa defended her. The cycle continued and it was tearing them apart as a family. Tucker slept on the couch, Alyssa slept alone, Brianna had a perpetually red cheek and Ashley cried herself to sleep, angry that her daddy didn't believe her.

When Alyssa is angry, she bakes. One day she was so upset that she couldn't stop crying so she decided to make a batch of muffins. Her mind was racing trying to find a way to resolve their family problems so she was having trouble focusing and accidentally dropped the muffin mix bowl on the floor. Batter splattered across the tile and on the cabinets. She reached for a towel to clean it up and then something happened that made her stop dead in her tracks. She was slapped across the face and slapped hard.

Alyssa couldn't move her body for the shock of what had happened. She was home alone but had felt a cold hand slap her left cheek just after having dropped the bowl of muffin batter.

When Tucker got home from work that evening she told him what happened. She was crying and trying to explain something that she really couldn't explain. Alyssa showed him her red cheek but by this point her face was a mess from crying and being so upset and she could tell he wasn't convinced that she was telling the truth. That instantly took her from confused and crying to angry and shouting. For over a week they had been fighting, the girls were scared to sleep in their room and now, in my mind, her husband was basically calling her a liar.

She snapped. She went out of her mind. They began screaming at each other at the top of their lungs. They said things, hurtful things that they had never dreamed of saying to each other before. This went on for a good ten to fifteen minutes and then Tucker said something that made her really lose it.

He said 'Go ahead, drop the bowl and prove to me that you got slapped.'

She was so enraged that she walked over and got the bowl out of the sink. It had been soaking with the other dishes so it was full of water. Alyssa grabbed it and threw it down on the floor. The water flew everywhere while the plastic bowl bounced away.

Tucker waited a second, scoffed and said, 'See, I knew it was a lie.'

But before she could respond, he watched as an invisible hand slapped her face so hard she turned almost a full one-hundred and eight degrees. Tucker's eyes were as big as saucers. He grabbed his wife and hugged and cried as he apologized.

Tears were pouring from Alyssa's face. She was confused, scared and physically hurt and then, as if on cue, someone knocked on the door.

Tucker answered the door to find their next door neighbor, Sandra. She had heard them arguing and was concerned. It was embarrassing but they decided that they couldn't blame her for checking on us.

Tucker told her that they were all right and she went back home. But that night, they were anything but all right. In truth, they were more dazed than anything, especially Alyssa. The only explanation she could come up with was they had a ghost who liked to slap people. So, they called the girls into the living room and asked them to tell them about the 'mean woman'.

Brianna told them that she has 'house rules' and is angry if they aren't followed. The 'mean woman' told her that nice girls don't wear silly socks, especially not to bed. She also said that dogs are dirty and should be kept outside.

Suddenly, as Brianna is talking, the room got really cold. Alyssa could see her eyes shift to her right and suddenly Brady came running into the living room. His hair was standing up on his hind end and his ears were forward like he's about to run after something.

Alyssa swallowed her next breath after Brianna said her next words, 'She's here. The mean woman is here.'

Tucker and Alyssa froze and waited for something to happen. Then, it did. Brianna tilted her head and asked, 'Mommy, did you drop a bowl on the floor?'

She could hear Tucker uttering beneath his breath in disbelief because they hadn't told the girls anything about what had happened that day. There's no way they could have known about her dropping the bowl.

Brianna then said, 'She says a woman should keep a tidy home.' Brianna looked down like she was pouting and said, 'She's means you, Mommy.'

Tucker and Alyssa just looked at each other, they didn't know what to think and had no idea what to say. Then Brianna looked around, smiles and say, 'She's gone now.'

To give you an idea on Alyssa's perspective at that time, she had never seen a ghost, had never really believed in ghosts and certainly didn't want to believe that her daughter was talking to one.

Tucker then suggested that they call his sister,

Lucy is a very spiritual, free thinking, kind of 'out there' person. The couple felt that if anyone they knew could point them in the right direction on what to do, she could. Lucy got the couple in touch with a psychic medium who came to the house and immediately connected with the 'mean woman'.

Before the psychic came, Alyssa had asked Brianna to describe the woman and she was blown away when the psychic's vision in her mind was identical to what her daughter had described.

Brianna had said that the 'mean woman' had dark hair, pulled into a tight bun. She wore a long, dark grey skirt and a white long sleeve shirt that was buttoned all the way up to her neck.

The psychic burned candles and incense while Tucker and Alyssa sat on the couch. They fully admit that they felt a little silly but were desperate to get rid of whatever was physically harming their family and bring them back together again.

They listened as the psychic explained to the unseen woman that she had passed away. Her time on earth was over and she was free to move on and join her loved ones. She used the term 'crossover' and described a white light and urged the mean woman to go into it. It only seemed like a few minutes had passed when the psychic turned and said, 'She's gone.'

Tucker and Alyssa weren't totally convinced that anything had really been accomplished but thanked the psychic and said goodbye.

As soon as the front door closed, Tucker said, 'Let's see if it worked.'

Alyssa looked at him and said "How?"

He shrugged his shoulders and said, "Drop a bowl."

Part of her was annoyed. I mean, he's not the one getting slapped, right? Another part of her was curious and wanted confirmation too. So, they went to the kitchen and filled a bowl with water and dropped it on the floor. She cringed, waiting for a slap, but nothing happened.

From that day forward the girls never had any terrifying visits from the 'mean woman'. Things went back to normal and they were once again a loving family.

It was probably three or four weeks later that Alyssa ran into her next door neighbor, Sandra. Obviously referring to the shouting she had heard when they were arguing, she asked if they were doing all right. Alyssa was vague and explained that they had gone through a rough time but things were back to normal.

Sandra said she was glad to hear that and that she didn't want to see Alyssa's family broken up like the previous owner's. She asked her what she meant by that and her answer left Alyssa speechless.

Sandra told her that the previous owners were newlyweds and only lived in the house for a few months when the husband was arrested for domestic abuse.

She said, "He would slap his wife so hard that she always had a bright red cheeks. It was so sad, they seemed so in love, too. Maybe even too much."

Alyssa asked her what she meant by that. Sandra told her that the wife would always defend her husband and say that he never hit her. But her father was not convinced and demanded that he be arrested.

Sandra then walked into her house and left Alyssa standing in her front yard, stunned and speechless. All she could think was did the previous owner really slap his wife or had the 'mean woman' tormented them like she had her family?

Alyssa started to cry. What if that had happened to her family? What is she or Tucker was accused of slapping their daughter? It was bad enough they thought it was Ashley but if the police got involved would they believe it was the ghost of a 'mean woman'?

Alyssa searched and searched for any record of a woman living in their home sometime in the past who may have been known to be strict but came up with nothing.

While she and her husband hope to never, ever have an experience like that again, they have learned to listen to their daughter and always stick together as a family.

Top 5 Things You Should Do While Visiting Tampa

Tampa, Florida was first visited by Spanish explorers in 1521. The curious travelers discovered the area to be a Native American fishing village by the name of *Tanpa*. Thanks to ancient and inaccurate cartographers, the name was eventually changed to Tampa. Not long after, a booming city was born.

Today, Tampa's population is well over 350,000 and has become a financial and commercial hub in addition to one of the world's most popular vacation destinations. Located in the Sunshine State, Tampa delivers on its official motto in abundance and offers an outdoor lifestyle that is second to none.

As a native of Tampa for over forty-five years, I am uniquely qualified to offer a "must see and do" list for those visiting the west coast of the Florida peninsula for some fun in the sun. I encourage you to experience each of the following exciting vacation experiences.

5: Fishing and boating

Contingent on your preference, you can choose between saltwater, freshwater and even deep-sea fishing. Tampa's waters boast over 200 species of fish including trout, snook and, of course, tarpon. The most popular fishing spot is off of the old Sunshine Skyway Bridge. You can use your own lures or opt to purchase live shrimp as bait to reel in snapper and redfish. More secluded spots can be found along the Courtney Campbell Causeway where top-water bait can bring in a prize-winning bass. The kids will enjoy hours of entertainment watching their bobbers dance on the waves. Ocean bottom catfish are lured to the bait and provide just enough resistance to challenge, yet reward, youngsters for their big catch of the day. There is no shortage of bait and tackle shops, and fishing equipment is readily available to rent. For those adventurous visitors, book a guide party and cast for tarpon and dolphin out in deeper waters.

There's nothing like a day on the water, relaxing and trolling the fish-filled waters around Tampa.

4: Busch Gardens, Zoo Tampa at Lowry Park and Adventure Island

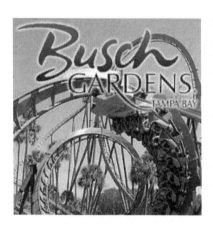

So much fun and exploration await you at Tampa's African themed park, Busch Gardens. The Dark Continent boasts nine roller coasters including *SheiKra*, which climbs 200 feet into the air and mercilessly falls downward at a pure ninety-degree drop. Two of the five thrill rides splash you through rapids of cool water to excite and refresh you under the warm Florida sun.

More than 12,000 animals representing 250 species that are indigenous to Africa can be safely observed throughout the park. Popular favorites include cheetahs, giraffes, chimpanzees, lions, tigers and gorillas.

When it's time to catch your breath from the speed of the speeding coasters, relax and visit Zoo Tampa at Lowry Park. Interact and support their rescued and rehabilitated animals from Elephants to rhinos to penguins. Zoo Tampa is a class act operation and committed to the care of their animals.

Ready to cool off? Adventure Island has exactly what you need to battle the heat of the Florida sun. Get ready for twists, turns, drops, and surprises as you spend the day having fun on all 10 adrenaline-fueled water slides. For those brave enough, there's a 17,000 foot wave pool while the more relaxed vacationer floats along the calming lazy river.

There is so much to see and do that you may not see everything in one day, but you will certainly have fun in your attempt to do so.

3: Shopping and entertainment

Channelside Tampa is a retail entertainment complex located in Downtown Tampa. Many begin and sometimes end the day at any of the numerous shopping and recreation options at the Bay Plaza.

For some culture, check out Paintings of the World and then discuss art with a stogie at Cigars by Antonio.

Next, dine on American, Asian, seafood, sushi or just grab a pizza. Numerous restaurants featuring cuisine from all around the world are available for lunch and dinner. Be sure to choose outdoor seating to fully appreciate the view of the adjacent water.

Don't forget to spend some time inside during the late afternoon at the Florida Aquarium. Revered as one of the top aquariums in the world, the Florida Aquarium is home to over 10,000 aquatic plant and animal life and also provides an outdoor water play-land for the kids.

There's plenty of fun to be had after dark too. Bring everyone to Splitsville, an upscale recreation center including bowling and pool tables for some friendly competition, food and drink.

If you're up for some traditional Irish fare and a beer, visit Maloney's Local Irish Pub. Be sure to visit them on the weekend and enjoy local live music.

Relax, take advantage of the valet services and enjoy your fun-filled day at Channelside Tampa.

If you're feeling lucky, don't forget to take a ride to the Seminole Hard Rock Hotel and Casino. Try your hand at poker, blackjack or slots. Enjoy a high-end buffet at Fresh Harvest and drinks at the center bar.

2: The Festivals and Outdoor Events at Curtis Hixon Waterfront Park

Eight acres comprise the Curtis Hixon Park as it stretches along the Hillsborough River in Downtown Tampa. Named for the 45th mayor of Tampa, the park hosts multiple events almost daily. A review of their online calendar will provide an array of scheduled events in which to participate.

Most weeks they offer at least one themed food festival. Dozens of local restaurants invite you to sample their food while you socialize and enjoy the beautiful warm weather.

There is typically a charity run on Saturdays, raising money for many important causes. Show up to run or simply cheer on the participants to show your support. Afterward, picnic with breakfast along the water and plan the remainder of your day under the rising sun.

Children's events are abundant as well. Many focus on healthy activities and provide stimulating games and build social skills among the young ones.

There are a plethora of annual events to choose from that range from Tampa Bay's Dragon Boat Race to Shakespeare in the Park and even an outdoor movie screening, proving that there is something for everyone at Curtis Hixon Waterfront Park.

1: Ybor City

If you're looking for rich history coupled with the sights and sounds of daytime activities and high energy nightlife, then historic Ybor City is the place for you.

Ybor City (pronounced "ee-bor") was founded in the 1880's by cigar manufacturers and is now home to residences and small businesses.

Park the car and let the streetcar safely transport you to the shops, multicultural restaurants and bars that occupy the extraordinary red brick buildings of another century.

Daytime shopping and dining options are plentiful on Ybor City's main thoroughfare, 7th Avenue. Pick up the pace with outdoor recreation activities or keep it low-key and casually peruse the historic statues in Centennial Park. There's even a resort and spa to remove your stress and help you relax before you head out for drinks.

Ybor City has indisputably become the destination of choice for Tampa's sizzling nightlife. Whether you prefer dance clubs, piano bars or the casual setting of drinks with friends while listening to an acoustic set in an intimate setting, Ybor City offers it all.

Rich with the cultures of its original population from Cuba, Italy and Spain, Ybor City boasts a unique charm that can only found in Tampa.

Welcome to Tampa and please enjoy your stay.

About the Author

Gare Allen is an independent author with books in several genres including paranormal, spiritual and humor and entertainment. His books can be found on amazon.com and you can follow him on Facebook and at www.gareallen.com

Contributors

Sam Baltrusis, author of "Ghosts of Boston," "Ghosts of Salem" and "13 Most Haunted in Massachusetts," is the former editor-in-chief of several regional publications including Spare Change News, Scout Somerville and Scout Cambridge. He has been featured as Boston's paranormal expert on the Biography Channel's "Haunted Encounters" and has been a featured speaker at various local venues, including the Massachusetts State House.

www.sambaltrusis.com

Joni Mayhan is a prolific author and paranormal investigator. She is the author of the Amazon.com best-selling "Bones in the Basement" and "Signs of Sprits". She conducts ghost walks and investigations in her home town of New Harmony, IN.

www.jonimayhan.com.

Please continue reading for a sample of First Impressions: True Tales from the Road – A Dog's Devotion

First Impressions: True Tales from the Road

A Dog's Devotion

When asked why I wanted to donate the net proceeds of *Haunted Tampa* to the HSCO Deputy Dogs, my response included two reasons:

First, we can never do enough to support the men and women of law enforcement. These individuals respond to dangerous and sometimes volatile situations and put their own safety on the line for strangers. They protect us and they help us and deserve nothing short of our complete respect and support.

Second, supporting their K-9 partners ensures they are healthy, trained and effective in keeping both their partners and the community safe from those who otherwise cause problems.

Like many of you reading this, I have an unmeasurable love of animals, particularly dogs. Below is a chapter from my book, First Impressions: True Tales from the Road in which I tell the story of a couple who relied heavily on their seeing-eye dogs and the love I was gifted to witness first-hand.

Not often enough, we are granted the opportunity to observe selfless kindness in the actions of loving and spirited people. During my second week of driving for a ride-sharing company, I accepted a ride that was timed at sixteen minutes but would last almost an hour.

Responding to a pick-up request at a Wal-Mart, I arrived to find a middle aged man and woman waiting in front of the exit doors with two full shopping carts of purchased goods, a microwave oven and a dog. I pulled up close to the curb and recognized the vest resting on the back of a beautiful, black Lab. She was a seeing-eye dog.

My heart sank instantly. My thoughts and feelings rushed back to a time a few years prior when I lost my black Lab mix, Sobek, to cancer at the age of eleven and half years.

Back in early 2001, the company I worked for began to liquidate their stores. My position as District Manager was removed but luckily I was kept on to close the stores in my surrounding area. No longer required to drive out of state and spend countless nights away from home, I was finally able to adopt a puppy and provide it the time and care it required. I awoke one Saturday morning and made my way to the local shelter. As if ordering a number four combo in a drive-thru, I asked for a black Lab puppy. The woman arched an eyebrow and replied that I was in luck as a litter of eight pups, just two months old, had just been dropped off.

For the next eleven and a half years, Sobek spent many warm Florida days swimming in the pool in endless pursuit of a floating and mostly, indestructible dog toy. Tired from hours of swimming and playing, he slept at the foot of my bed, every night.

While my responsibilities as a driver included tasks specifically behind the wheel, my duties as a fellow human being to those who may require assistance knew few limits. I parked the car and greeted the couple. The intelligent Lab moved the woman to the car door and she very capably found the handle. I turned my attention to the man who seemed to have a similar sight disability but to a slightly lesser degree. Regardless, I assisted and placed the abundant bags of food and household items into my trunk. It took some time but the carts were emptied and I wedged the microwave oven behind my seat with the gentleman beside it.

Once back in the car, I found the woman seat-belted in the passenger seat with the black Lab at her feet; only her big, brown inquisitive Labrador eyes peering up at me.

Having worked in the pet industry, I knew the rules and so did the dog. While wearing the vest, she was working and was not to be approached or touched from anyone besides her handler. I therefor resisted my urge to reach out and scratch her adorable muzzle.

The woman began a direct, verbal exchange with the man in the backseat.

"Do you have the microwave?"

The man's arm was resting on the large metal oven as he replied. "Yup, right here."

"We got a good deal on the display model." The woman proudly bragged to me.

"Did you pick up the prescriptions?" The woman asked turning her attention back to her companion.

"Yes, all of them." He replied. In anticipation of her follow up question, he stated, "And, I confirmed our appointment with the doctor tomorrow at eleven a.m."

Satisfied that her mental checklist had been reviewed, the woman beamed a wide, pleased smile. "You take such good care of me."

The man nodded and countered with, "We take care of each other."

Despite their short conversation, their love was palpable. I instantly understood their strong commitment to one another as they worked together to ensure each other's well-being.

Directed by the GPS in my phone, I began the drive to the couple's home and couldn't help but recall Sobek as I glanced down at the loving, curious eyes of the dog. Without being asked, I told the woman about Sobek and my wonderful time with him. In response, she began to describe some of the service dogs that she had owned during her life. There may have been more, but she told me of four.

While it made sense after hearing it, I had not realized that the owners would keep the seeing-eye dogs after their service time had ended. Indeed, they are very much their pets, despite their servitude. I guess I assumed that they either were service dogs for their entire life or they went up for adoption after their service time ended; no longer of use to the individual in need of their assistance. My assumption was another limited, small-minded moment.

Her lab remained still for the duration of the ride. I continued to resist the urge to rub that greying muzzle with my hand and respected the request clearly printed on her vest.

The woman described her past service dogs in fond reflection. Her first was also a Lab, but a yellow male called, Sammy. He had since passed away at the age of thirteen. Unfortunately, the bigger dogs often don't have the longevity of life that the smaller dogs possess. Next, was a small Samoyed mix called, Shadow. She described a fluff of hair atop short legs that she was told was white as snow. Her most recently retired dog was a Golden Retriever named Daisy. An extremely smart dog, she told me that Daisy would, without fail, anticipate her needs without command. Finally, she introduced the pooch at her feet, Sugar. At the mention of her name, her big, brown, expectant eyes turned to her handler and awaited direction.

During my almost twelve years in the pet industry, I learned a great deal about animal care. In fact, that was literally part of my position's title. The majority of the company's business was generated from the dog food and supplies departments. That dictated that the bulk of the internal training would be focused on canine care.

The best part of my job was touring stores and meeting the visiting pet parents and their canine companions. With three dogs of my own during my time in the industry, my heart carved a very large space for their well-being. Admittedly, I struggled with the use of dogs as service animals. On one side, I understood the benefit of their training and the use of their minds to mitigate the disability of their owner. In the case of my passenger, Sugar led her safely through crowded stores to deter her from tripping or walking into a display or other people. Sugar was very much her eyes and she trusted her implicitly.

Alternately, I wondered about the quality of life of a typical service-dog. Sugar was a healthy looking, two-year old Lab with a shiny coat and clean, white teeth. She appeared very well cared for, but what of her needs outside of her role? I had learned that dogs require more than just food and water. Exercise and socialization are paramount in fostering a happy, well-behaved and responsive pet. Additionally, we cannot forget the specific function of the domesticated breed that we, by design, instilled in them.

For example, while playing fetch with certain breeds is an hour or so of fun for us, it is behaviorally vital to those breeds named for that purpose. Sugar is a Labrador Retriever. Her very name defines her singular focus. Labs are social and loving and very much the perfect pack dog. They are too happy to be in charge and too big and strong to bring up the rear. Finding their comfort zone in the middle of the pack, they are known to thrive mentally and psychologically while in the frequent company of other dogs.

My personal opinions whirling through my mind ended when we arrived to the couple's home. I backed the car up to their door as instructed. The woman found her way out of my car and, with Sugar's direction, up the rock walkway to her front door. After shuffling his way along the same path, the man retrieved a rolling cart from inside the house and slowly wheeled it to the trunk. He filled it with his bags and my offer to carry the microwave oven inside was graciously accepted. I walked into their home and placed the oven on a kitchen counter top. The house was dark and I could barely see. All of the window treatments were closed but after a second or two, my brain understood the why.

I turned to say good-bye and found the woman standing beside her sofa with a broad smile on her face as she asked me if I would like to meet her pups.

Yes, please!

With one command, three dogs came running into the home from the opened backdoor. First was Shadow, the fluffy Samoyed mix. He found his way to me instantly and barked playfully at my feet. The Golden Retriever and Lab, Daisy and Sugar, entered as a pair. Sugar had apparently made quick use of the backyard for a bathroom break and was reunited with her retriever gal-pal. After a quick sniff around me they launched themselves into playful glee in the couple's living room. With her vest removed, Sugar was now off the clock and indulging her breed's social inclination to play with her fellow retriever. Big, healthy, active dog noises filled the house. The joy beamed from the woman's face as she listened to the soft, playful growls and howling barks of the dogs while they tussled about her living room.

It was abundantly clear that when they wore their vests, they intently, loyally and solely worked for her. The dogs provided her care and direction while ensuring safety and support. When the vests were removed, they were full throttle dogs. The woman fostered a loving home where the pups played and were well cared for in exchange for their love and support. Watching the woman beam with joy at the sounds of her playful pack, it was obvious that she loved them, whether they were at work or play.

I turned and noticed that the man was feeling his way through his kitchen as he put away the groceries. He carefully felt and identified each item and ran his fingers along the cabinets until he found its place. I observed that only the bottom shelves were utilized and the newly purchased, unopened boxes of food were placed behind opened ones.

The woman felt her way along the back of the couch until she found herself in front of the sofa and sat in what I assumed was her favorite and familiar spot. She raised both her arms and cupped her hands in front of her. I watched, unsure as to what she was doing. Within seconds, the man, smiling ear to ear, presented her with a hot cup of tea that he had warmed in the recently purchased microwave. The woman boasted a wide smile at retrieving her beverage and her glee illuminated the darkened room.

"Thank you, Sweetie." She sang as she smelled the aroma wafting from her cup.

"My pleasure, baby." The man replied and felt his way back to the kitchen to continue putting the groceries away.

I wondered how many times he had prepared for her a cup of tea. A hundred? A thousand? Yet, the act was still executed with his loving pleasure and she continued to find joy in a simple, hot drink.

It stood to reason that their quality of life and safety was dependent on routine regarding where they walk, sit and place their personal items. However, their care and love for each other and their pets demonstrated a deep affection that I believe was primarily performed out of love, rather than necessity.

Sugar broke free of the rough-housing long enough for me to finally scratch her slightly grey muzzle. I saw my own Lab in her big, brown eyes and my own watered at the overwhelming display of the couple's devotion to each other and the sweet, unconditional love and support of their dogs.

You've just read chapter three of <u>First Impressions: True Tales From The Road</u> by Gare Allen.

Made in the USA
Columbia, SC
05 January 2021